The Reality of Jesus

The Reality of Jesus

An Essay in Christology

Dermot A. Lane

Veritas Publications and Sheed & Ward
Dublin and London

First published 1975 by
Veritas Publications
7-8 Lower Abbey Street
Dublin 1
&
Sheed & Ward Ltd
2 Creechurch Lane
London EC3A 5AQ

Reprinted 1986

Nihil obstat
Richard Sherry DD
Censor Deputatis

Imprimatur
✠ Dermot
Archbishop of Dublin
21 August 1975

The *nihil obstat* and *imprimatur* are declarations
that a text is considered to be free of doctrinal or moral
error. They do not necessarily imply agreement with
opinions expressed by the author.

ISBN 0 901810 85 1

Cover design by Eddie McManus
Printed in Great Britain by A. Wheaton & Co. Ltd, Exeter

Contents

I Introduction

The current renewal taking place in theology could be summed up in terms of a return to the origins of Christianity. This going back to the beginnings brings us into direct contact with the person of Jesus Christ. As a result theology once again is rediscovering its christological base. This can be seen in the present-day theology of faith, the Church, the sacraments, and the last things, each of which take their inspiration from the reality of Jesus. Our acceptance and appropriation of the mystery of Jesus Christ is something that determines our attitude towards everything else within Christianity. In particular our response to the person of Jesus Christ shapes and informs our approach to the ultimate mystery in life which we call God.

In these times when literally nothing is left unquestioned it is not enough to merely assume or to assert the importance of Jesus Christ. Instead the reality of Jesus, like everything else, must be examined, exposed, and vindicated. The historical foundations and the theological content of the mystery of Jesus Christ must be critically assessed and worked out in the light of modern developments. This book sets out to do just that.

The mystery of Jesus Christ

The mystery of Christ is the story of the life, death and resurrection of Jesus. For the sake of convenience the full mystery of Jesus Christ can be broken down into two parts. These are what is commonly called (a) the Christ-Event, and (b) the universal significance of that event for under-

standing life itself. As such the mystery of Jesus Christ is
not something that suddenly came into view out of nowhere
at a particular point in time. Rather the mystery of Jesus
Christ is a reality that took hundreds of years to fully
unfold itself into a clearly defined framework. It is within
this growth period of Christian experience and theological
reflection that we situate the successive stages of the Christ-
Event and its universal significance. A brief description of
each of these stages will help to understand the rich range
of the full mystery of Jesus Christ.

The expression "the Christ-Event" is a type of short-
hand summarising the theological significance of the
historical life, death, and resurrection of Jesus. The
Christ-Event itself is composed of a historical experience
and a theological understanding of that particular experience. The historical side of the Christ-Event consists in the
given fact that a man called Jesus of Nazareth appeared
two thousand years ago within the history of Judaism.
The theological significance of this fact is to be found
in the confession that this Jesus of Nazareth is the definitive
visitation of God to mankind in history.

This description of the Christ-Event goes back to the
historical experience and the theological understanding of
the life, death and resurrection of Jesus by the apostles.
This experience and understanding is summed up in the
simple formula "Jesus Christ". The Jesus part of this
formula refers to the historical side of the Christ-Event
whereas the Christ part embraces the theological significance of this given fact.

Unfortunately popular usage has tended to employ
the word "Christ" as a proper name for Jesus of Nazareth
whereas in primitive Christianity the word "Christ" was a
title designating a specific function within the socio-religious
traditions of Judaism.[1] A more accurate way therefore of
using this formula would be to talk of Jesus who is called
the Christ or Jesus who is the Christ or simply Jesus
as Christ.

INTRODUCTION 11

Traces of this more primitive and correct usage can be found in the New Testament. For instance the confession of Peter at Caesarea Philippi brings this out: "But who do you say that I am?" Peter answered him: "You are the Christ" (*Mk 8:29*).[2] Again the same point can be found in the first sermon of Peter: "Let all the house of Israel therefore know assuredly that God has made him both Lord and Christ (theological dimension), this Jesus whom you crucified (historical side)" *Acts 2:36-38*. Even as late as the nineties of the first century we are told that the gospel of John was "written that you may believe that Jesus is the Christ" (*Jn 20:31*).

To acknowledge Jesus as the Christ is to acknowledge him as the messiah, the "anointed one of Yahweh" whom the prophets foretold and the Jewish world eagerly awaited. This proclamation "Jesus as the Christ" signalled the irrevocable ending of one era and the certain beginning of another era.[3] The confession of Jesus as the Christ became "the primary faith formula"[4] of early Christianity and "the crystallisation point of all other New Testament christological viewpoints".[5]

Another early formulation of the Christ-Event is to be found in the confession that "Jesus is Lord". Again this formula is made up of a historical fact (Jesus) and a theological reality (Lord). Quite clearly the kerygma, the good news of the early Church, consisted in the proclamation of the fact that "Jesus is Lord". Paul expresses this succinctly in *Rom 10:9*: "If you confess that Jesus is Lord and believe that God raised him from the dead you will be saved from your sins."[6] In all probability it was this confession of Jesus as Lord that constituted the first creed within infant Christianity. To this extent the Christ-Event may be summed up as that area of christology which is concerned with the exposition of the historical foundations and the theological significance of the confession that Jesus is Lord.

It is important that a proper balance be maintained

between the historical and theological dimensions of the Christ-Event. To ignore the historical side of the Christ-Event would be to deny the basic assertion that Jesus identified himself historically with the human condition of mankind. This would give rise to the theological heresies known as Docetism and Gnosticism both of which deny the real humanity of Jesus.[7] On the other hand to neglect the theological side of the Christ-Event leads to the opposite errors of Moralism and Adoptionism which play down the divinity of Jesus.[8]

It is out of these early confessions concerning Jesus of Nazareth that the universal significance of the Christ-Event emerged. If the man Jesus is confessed as the Christ and Lord then this must have implications for our understanding of God, man, and the universe. It is these implications of the Christ-Event that bring out what we call the universal significance of Jesus. In this way the universal significance of the Christ-Event provides us with a new way of looking at the meaning of life. It is these different dimensions of the mystery of Jesus Christ which must be taken up and worked out if we are to provide an adequate and comprehensive christology for today. The first half of this book will concentrate on the Christ-Event whereas the latter half will focus upon the universal significance of the Christ-Event.

It should be clear from this introduction that the mystery of Jesus Christ has a background as well as a progressive history of growth and doctrinal development. The background to the Christ-Event is something that is rooted in the thought forms and world view of the Jewish people stretching back into the history of Israel and Juda. It would be impossible in a book of this kind to map out all the details that belong to this Jewish background of the Christ-Event. However at the risk of over-simplification certain elementary notions should be mentioned at this early stage which must be taken for granted. Prominent here is the Jewish faith understanding of Yahweh as a reality present to his people in and through the events of history. For the Jews Yahweh was active in the world, moulding and shaping their historical destiny according to a particular plan and purpose. Behind this faith understanding lay the presence of a uniquely original conception of history as a phenomenon that unfolded itself progressively within a linear, as distinct from cyclic, mode of development under the direction of Yahweh.[9] The realisation of this plan and purpose gradually disclosed itself through a series of different historical events in which Yahweh was actively present. These included first of all the gathering of a people,[10] followed by the constituting of them as a nation, the liberating of them from slavery through the exodus event, the leading of them to the promised land and the drawing up of a covenant relationship between them and Yahweh. Within this historical process prophets played a prominent part by reminding people of their covenant relationship with Yahweh.

In particular Yahweh emerged as the God of promises.[11] In time these promises became centred around the establishment of the kingdom of God upon earth. The leading figure here was the messiah who would be associated with the setting up of the Kingdom of God. From this fact there arose a series of different messianic expectations. In the end it would be through the messiah that the specific mode of God's presence in history, man's place in the world, and the ultimate destiny of the universe would be revealed through the inauguration of God's Kingdom. It is against this type of background that the Christ-Event came into being. Within the following chapters we will map out the historical foundations of the Christ-Event, unravel its implications, and discover its universal significance for our understanding of God, man and the universe.

Different approaches to the mystery of Christ

Now that we are clear about the basic terms of reference within the mystery of Jesus Christ we must ask what is the most suitable approach to the study of christology. The question of method in christology is a relatively recent one. Indeed the possibility of alternative approaches to the mystery of Jesus Christ has only arisen in this century due to the progress made by biblical research.

The traditional approach to christology began by acknowledging the universal significance of the Christ-Event as defined by the early councils of Nicea (321), Ephesus (431) and Chalcedon (451). These councils found their classical formulation in the dogma of the Incarnation that stated "God became man in Jesus of Nazareth". Acceptance of the dogma of the Incarnation became the basic starting point within traditional christology. This dogma determined the direction of everything else in christology. As a result the messiahship, the divinity, and the pre-existence of Jesus were automatically implied in the doctrine of the Incarnation.

This approach is now popularly described as a "high christology" or a "descending christology" or a "christology from above", for the rather obvious reasons that it emphasises the exalted or high quality of Jesus.[12] The underlying spirit of this christology was one in which the eternal Son of God came down from heaven and became man in Jesus of Nazareth in order to redeem mankind from its sinful condition. Because Jesus had a divine and human nature he could represent both God and man and therefore he could bring man back to God. Within this scheme of things the different events within the life of the historical Jesus were interpreted as illustrations of the Incarnation.[13] As a result incidents like the temple story, the theophany at the baptism of Jesus, the transfiguration, the miracle stories and the resurrection were all read through the eyes of the Incarnation in traditional christology.

This approach to the mystery of Jesus Christ goes back ultimately to the gospel of John which in fact has a high christology. However it was at the Council of Nicea in 321 with its declaration of Jesus as "of one substance" with the Father that exclusive concentration on a high christology came into being. The occasion of this definition was the teaching of Arius who appeared to deny the divinity of Jesus by viewing him as half god and half man. It has been said that the Church never fully recovered from its reaction against Arius. This is certainly true in regard to the influence that the Council of Nicea had upon method in christology. From the fourth century onwards the mystery of Jesus Christ has always been approached from a high Nicean point of view.

This can be seen in the two famous schools of Alexandrian and Antiochene christology of the fourth and fifth centuries. Both began with high christologies taking the Word/*Logos* as their point of departure. The Alexandrian School began with the principle that the Word/*Logos* assumed flesh/*sarx* while the Antiochenes stressed that the Word/*Logos* became man/*anthropos*.[14] Thereafter these schools went their different ways. The Alexandrian emphasised the divinity of Jesus whereas the Antiochene, while acknowledging the reality of the Word, brought out the importance of the humanity of Jesus. In both cases, however, the starting point is the same : that of a descending Word from above. This basic incarnational approach has continued down through the ages in varying shades right into the present century. As a result traditional christology with some exceptions has been heavily weighted in the direction of the divinity of Jesus.

Since the turn of this century however there has been a growing concern among christologists about the possibility of initiating an alternative approach to the mystery of Jesus Christ. This concern has been stimulated by the presence of certain difficulties in the traditional patterns of christology. These difficulties have come to the fore with increasing persuasiveness in this century. The area most responsible for focusing upon these problems in traditional christology could be summed up in terms of "the influence of history". This "influence of history" touches upon such central issues as historical research into the gospels,[15] the historical character of revelation[16] and the historicity of doctrinal expression.[17] Each of these areas as we shall see raises questions for traditional christology. As a result of these questions the more specific question of method in regard to the mystery of Jesus Christ has become a matter of considerable discussion.[18] Within this discussion certain misgivings emerge with regard to the traditional approach to the mystery of Jesus Christ.

It is pointed out that a christology from above tends to take for granted the divinity of Jesus Christ whereas in fact one of the basic tasks of christology is to present good reasons for confessing Jesus to be true God and true man. Recent phenomena like the Jesus People and the Rock Opera *Jesus Christ—Superstar* clearly indicate that we can no longer presume on general acceptance of divinity in speaking of Jesus Christ. In a word, to begin with the doctrine of the Incarnation appears to beg the basic question that christology should set out to establish.[19]

Furthermore it is noted that by concentrating on the divinity of Jesus there is a real danger of blanketing the fundamental importance and significance of the humanity of Jesus. This danger is evidenced by the persistent presence of Monophysitism[20] in the minds of many Christians in regard to their understanding of Jesus.

Similarly by starting christology on the premise that God became man in Jesus one is starting with an *a priori* abstract notion of God. In practice this concept of God is taken from natural theology or the Old Testament and then projected on to Jesus of Nazareth. A not untypical example of this can be found in the traditional understanding of the qualities of God as omnipotent and omniscient. Such qualities are taken and imposed upon traditional christology in such a way that Jesus is expected to be omnipotent and omniscient throughout his life. Within the plan of revelation, however, it is supposed to be the man Jesus who gives us our true understanding of God.

In reality of course one would have to stand in the position of God himself if one were to properly follow the way of his Son from above into the world.[21]

In addition a christology in which the Incarnation predominates as a starting point tends to relegate the mystery of the resurrection to a position of secondary importance. In such a christology the resurrection appears simply as the outcome of the Incarnation of the eternal Son of God.[22]

In the light of these difficulties which are present, in varying degrees, in certain forms of traditional christology, there has been a search for other approaches to the mystery of Jesus Christ. The most obvious choice would be to begin christology from the other end, concentrating on the man Jesus giving rise to what is called a "low christology" which starts "from below". This alternative has opened up interesting possibilities producing a whole set of new categories such as Jesus "the man for others",[23] "the revolutionary",[24] "the outsider",[25] "the Way",[26] "the representative",[27] and "the harlequin".[28]

Unfortunately however this extreme reaction leaves itself open to a reversal of the charges brought against traditional high christologies. The divinity of Jesus is taken over by his humanity, Monophysitism gives way to Moralism, revelation becomes reductionist, resurrection replaces incarnation, and Adoptionism absorbs Docetism. The final result is a standing of Nicea on its head.

An exclusively low christology therefore is not a viable alternative to the excesses of an exclusively high christology. The real difficulty with low christologies is that they never get off the ground, becoming boxed in by their own preoccupations. Yet in spite of these dangers the underlying inspiration of a low christology is attractive in that it provides a new point of departure for approaching the mystery of Jesus Christ. To this extent there is no reason why one could not adopt a low christology as one's starting point and then proceed to allow this starting point to be drawn in whatever direction one's study of the Christian sources dictates. In other words a third possibility would seem to present itself here that would steer a middle course between the two extremes of a closed low christology and a rigidly high christology. This third possibility could reasonably call itself a low-ascending christology.

Such a low-ascending approach to the mystery of Jesus Christ would seem to be a real option today within christology. For one thing it would bring the mystery of Jesus Christ into the main stream of theology which has become inductive rather than deductive. In addition it would relocate christology into the living stream of revelation as historical and experiential.[29] Most of all a low-ascending christology reinstates the mystery of Jesus Christ in its original biblical context where it properly belongs. Within this original context biblical research would seem to suggest that the New Testament christology itself began with the man Jesus.[30] Evidence for this can be found in early biblical christologies such as: "Let all the House of Israel therefore know assuredly that God has made him both Lord and Christ, this Jesus whom you crucified" (*Acts 2:36*). It is this primitive pattern that gave rise to the more developed christologies of *Phil 2:5-11* and *Jn 1:1-14*. Within this low-ascending christology the dogma of the Incarnation would appear not as a starting point but as a conclusion to one's examination of the basic sources.

For these reasons we propose to adopt a low-ascending christology in our investigation of the mystery of Jesus Christ. In practical terms this means beginning with the man Jesus through a process of historical enquiry that will lead to an understanding of the confession of Jesus as Christ and Lord and a discovery of its subsequent universal implications.

2   The historical Jesus and biblical research

In deciding to adopt a low-ascending christology we have committed ourselves to the task of trying to get back to the historical foundations of the Christ-Event as centred around the life of the man Jesus. This task, as we shall discover, involves much more than simply just reading off the life of Jesus from the gospels as we know them today.

The secular sources for the life of Jesus provide us with very little information. Neutral observers like Josephus the historian (c.93 A.D.), Pliny the younger (c.110 A.D.), Tacitus (c.116 A.D.), and Suetonius (c.120 A.D.), do testify to the historical existence of Jesus but they give us no details about the life of Jesus. This independent evidence for the actual existence of Jesus is useful but it does not bring us very far in trying to get back to the historical foundations of the Christ-Event.

The most important source for the life of Jesus is the New Testament, especially the gospels. When one turns to the gospels, however, one discovers that they do not give us an historical account, strictly speaking, of the life of Jesus in terms of providing a chronological record of what happened. Instead the gospels present us primarily with a faith-picture of the early Church's experience and understanding of Jesus who is the Christ and the risen Lord. The gospels were written by men of faith for men of faith. They are the end product of a long process of reflection on the life of Jesus stretching over a period of thirty-three to sixty-five years. Thus they provide us with a delicately balanced combination of history and theology, facts and

19

faith, events and interpretation of events. They are therefore complex documents which cannot simply be taken
up and read in the way we might read a modern book
in history. They do not set out to give us a biography of
Jesus in the ordinary sense of that word.

Consequently a certain sensitivity towards the complex nature of the gospels is required when one is trying
to get back to the historical foundations of the Christ-
Event. It was the need for such sensitivity that gave rise
to the quest of the historical Jesus and its continuing
presence in modern christology. A review of these different
attempts to go back behind the gospels to the life of Jesus
will help to introduce us to the problem involved in seeking out the historical foundations of the Christ-Event.
In particular it will alert us against the extremes that
should be avoided in trying to ground the Christ-Event
in history.

The quest of the historical Jesus

Up to the end of the eighteenth century there was no
apparent need for any sensitivity towards the complex
nature of the gospels. It was generally assumed that the
New Testament gave a clear and accurate account of the
life of the historical Jesus. It was also taken for granted
that the proclaimed Christ and Lord of the early Church
was a replica of the earthly Jesus. Further it was presumed
that an exact one-for-one correspondence existed between
history and theology, between facts and faith, between
events and interpretation of events, as set out in the gospels.

Suddenly these suppositions were radically called into
question by a German Professor of oriental languages
called Herman S. Reimarus (d.1768). He claimed that
the gospel accounts had smothered the life of the historical
Jesus in supernatural dogmas. "Back from the Christ of
dogma to the real Jesus" barked Reimarus. Thus was born
the problem of the historical Jesus. A wedge was driven

between the historical Jesus and the Christ of the gospels. A road block was set up on the traditional highway between Jesus and Christ or what is now called the Jesus of history and the Christ of faith.

The immediate response to Reimarus was one of indignation. The thesis that it was impossible to find the real Jesus of the Gospel was unacceptable. To counter it a whole series of different lives of Jesus mushroomed all over Europe in the nineteenth century, especially in Germany. Different authors attempted to portray in biographical form the life of Jesus, giving rise to a movement known as "the liberal quest of the historical Jesus".

This liberal quest of the historical Jesus created confusion and chaos. The nineteenth-century biographers became "like plastic surgeons making over the face of their patient in their own image, or like an artist who projects himself into the figure he creates".[1] Thus Jesus was portrayed as "a fanatic, a pious sufferer . . . , a social benefactor, a moral example, and a religious leader".[2] In the end these lives of Jesus became "more like novels than biographies".[3] The result of this rash of lives was scepticism about the possibility of ever reaching the real historical Jesus due to the multiplicity of different pictures being produced.

The final death-knell was sounded by Albert Schweitzer in his important work *On the Quest of the Historical Jesus* published at the turn of the century. Schweitzer buried effectively the liberal quest of the historical Jesus in terms of total failure. The historical Jesus, it now appeared, could not be recovered scientifically from the gospel material. Scepticism concerning the historical foundations of Christianity became the order of the day with Christian faith assuming total independence from critical investigation of the New Testament.

The next major figure to appear on the scene around the time of World War I was Rudolph Bultmann (1884-). Briefly Bultmann held that the most we can know with

absolute certainty about the historical Jesus is that he
existed and that he died on a cross. We must assert the
givenness (*dass*) of Jesus but as for the how (*wie*) and the
what (*was*) of this life there can be no certainty.[4] Bultmann's
primary concern was to protect the independence of Christian faith from the changing results of historical research.
As far as he was concerned Christian faith had no need
of any historical scaffolding.

In retrospect it could be argued that Bultmann's position was an advance on the deadlock reached by the old
liberal quest. At least he seemed to anchor the Christ-
Event in history even though we know nothing about the
details of this particular history. In spite of this apparent
progress, however, an underlying mistrust concerning the
historical foundations of Christianity remained. Bultmann's
position became very influential in Europe and was accepted
in varying sceptical shades by many leading Protestant
theologians of the day like Barth, Brunner, Tillich, and
Gogarten.

In the early fifties a new programme addressed to
the question of the historical Jesus was initiated by a group
of theologians in Germany known as the Post-Bultmannians.[5] The approach was called the "new" quest of
the historical Jesus: "new" in order to distinguish itself
from the old liberal quest which had concentrated on
producing a biography of Jesus.[6] Broadly speaking the new
questers initially at least held that it was possible to disentangle the historical Jesus from the gospel material
and that there was therefore no need to accept the scepticism of Bultmann and company. They also went on to
point out that there was a basic continuity between the
historical Jesus and the proclaimed Christ of the gospels.
These are some of the more positive points amongst the
Post-Bultmannians about which most members of the movement were in agreement at least in the early stages. As time
went on, however, this area of agreement amongst the new
questers became smaller and smaller. For some it was

"the words" of Jesus that became all-important. For others it was merely "the deeds". In both cases there developed a tendency to return to the nineteenth-century quest by being over-concerned with the life of the historical Jesus.[7] This return led to the suggestion that the Resurrection and Pentecostal experiences add nothing new to the content of Christian faith.[8]

In the middle sixties yet another grouping emerged calling itself the Pannenberg Circle. This consisted of a small gathering of theologians led by the increasingly influential Wolfhart Pannenberg (1928-   ). Pannenberg and his followers take for granted the more positive points which we have mentioned among the Post-Bultmannians. After that there is sharp disagreement between the Pannenberg group and the Post-Bultmannians, especially on matters relating to the importance of the resurrection for understanding the Christ-Event. For Pannenberg, who is now working more and more on his own, the main context in which the life of the historical Jesus took place is that of an apocalyptic expectation. By an apocalyptic expectation Pannenberg simply means an horizon in which the end of time in terms of judgment and resurrection is about to take place. Within this specifically Jewish context of apocalyptic expectation the resurrection of Jesus is of paramount importance and is essential to a right understanding of the Christ-Event.[9]

This short survey on the quest of the historical Jesus opens up for us some of the issues involved in trying to get back to the historical foundations of the Christ-Event. It also highlights the fact that the problem of the historical Jesus is ultimately a question concerning biblical research and a right understanding of the special character of the gospel material.

An emerging consensus within biblical research

Our discussion so far has centred around the contours of a debate that was taking place primarily in Protestant circles. The reason for this is that the problem of the historical Jesus only came into being with the discovery of the new science of historical research and its application to the New Testament. It was the Protestant tradition that first took over this new science, developed it, and applied it courageously to biblical revelation. Today however biblical historical research and the problem of the historical Jesus are as much Catholic issues as Protestant ones.

Biblical research may be described as the application of the "historical method" to the Bible. It came into being in the nineteenth century, having its origins in the enlightenment period of the eighteenth century. It was occasioned by an overly inflated understanding of revelation at that time.[10] In its infancy biblical research appeared to take on a destructive role producing extreme forms of naturalism, rationalism, and scepticism towards the scriptures. This was due in no small measure to the pressure of positivistic principles in the philosophy of its earlier proponents. Gradually, however, through a process of maturation what began under a dark cloud of suspicion came to be universally accepted as an indispensable instrument for understanding the complex character of the scriptures.

The initial response of the Catholic church to the movement of biblical research was one of reserve and even outright rejection at times. With the passage of time, however, and the refinement of its methodology the Catholic church gradually came around to accepting the principles of historical research. The major breakthrough came in 1943 with the publication of the encyclical *Divino Afflante Spiritu* by Pius XII, which gave the green light to Catholic scholars to use the methods of biblical research. This opened up a whole new area of biblical studies within Catholicism. This encyclical was followed by an equally significant document published by the Pontifical Biblical Commission in 1964 entitled *The Historical Truth of the Gospels* Unfortunately the appearance of this most important instruction

from Rome was overshadowed by the events of the Second
Vatican Council at the time. These developments in turn
were further endorsed by the Constitution on Revelation
which came out from the Second Vatican Council in 1965.[11]

A brief outline of the 1964 Instruction from Rome
and subsequent developments will help us to piece together
the emergence of a common consensus concerning the
direction of biblical research amongst Catholic and Protestant scholars alike. This consensus will introduce us to
the true context in which the problem of the historical Jesus
arises and it will also provide us with the necessary critical
tools for going back behind the gospels to the historical
foundations of the Christ-Event.

The 1964 Instruction points out that there are "three
stages of tradition"[12] behind the gospels as we know them
today. There are first of all the original words and deeds
of the historical Jesus which were delivered according to
"the methods of reasoning and exposition which were in
common use at the time".[13] The second layer of tradition
is made up of the oral proclamation by the apostles of the
life, death and resurrection of Jesus. Here the instruction
talks about "the fuller understanding"[14] that the apostles
have of the words and deeds of the historical Jesus in the
light of the Resurrection and Pentecostal experiences. It also
acknowledges the presence of different literary forms within
this second type of tradition such as "catechesis, narratives,
testimonies, hymns, doxologies, prayers".[15] The third layer
consists in the compilation of this apostolic preaching into
the written form of the gospels as we know them today.
This arrangement of the gospels, it is pointed out, took
place according to "the peculiar purpose" of each evangelist and involved a process of selection, synthesis and
explicitation.[16] The instruction sums up this part of its
commentary on the different layers of tradition by reminding us of the importance of taking into consideration the
origin and composition of the gospels as well as making
due use of "the legitimate findings of recent research"

if we are to appreciate fully what the authors are saying.[17]

The most significant thing about this instruction is the calm way in which it openly admits that what we have in the written gospels is not the words and deeds of Jesus in the first stage of tradition nor even in the form in which they were preached in the second stage of tradition, but only in the form in which they were finally edited by the evangelists.[18] This admission clearly highlights the necessity of going back behind the written gospels if we are to rediscover the historical foundations of the Christ-Event. Indeed the need to do this as implied in the instruction would seem to strengthen our decision to adopt a low-ascending christology in trying to formulate the full mystery of Jesus Christ. The possibility of going back through the different layers of tradition is now quite real in view of the advances of biblical research in this century. In fact biblical research has developed into three distinct areas which correspond broadly speaking to the three different layers of tradition in the gospels.

The first layer of tradition in the gospels is made accessible through the science of "historical criticism". It was this historical criticism that gave rise to the quest of the historical Jesus which we have already outlined above. The second layer of tradition is discovered through the method of "form criticism". This method came into being in Germany between the first and second world wars. It concerned itself with the formation of the gospel tradition which took place between the years thirty-three to sixty-five A.D. (e.g. the literary forms of catechesis and doxologies referred to by the Instruction). The third layer of tradition is studied through the techniques of "redaction history" which has only come into being since the middle fifties. Redaction criticism concentrates on discovering the dominant ideas which determined the final editing of the gospels as we know them today (e.g. the "peculiar purpose" of each evangelist mentioned by the Instruction). These three areas of biblical research corresponding to the three layers of tradition in the gospels are now accepted by most Christian scholars.

In addition to this broad consensus, progress has also been made concerning the meaning of history within biblical research as it relates to the first layer of tradition in the gospel material. One of the factors that bedevilled the old quest of the historical Jesus was the question of what constituted history. Since the quest of the historical Jesus developed under the influence of the enlightenment period there arose a certain conception of history that was strongly coloured by positivistic principles. These principles produced a hard distinction between cold naked facts that exist "back there" in the past which can be verified (*historie*) and the particular existential meaning and interpretation that these facts can be given (*geschichte*). This distinction between facts and interpretation of facts has been challenged by some of the post-Bultmannians and in particular by Wolfhart Pannenberg. It is pointed out that such a crude dichotomy is no longer acceptable. Instead a more unified vision is proposed.

This unified vision sees history as the meaningful manifestation of reality as it appears at a particular point in time. As such, history cannot be reduced merely to a clinical observation of what happened in the past. Rather, history is the unfolding of meaningfully interpreted events in a way that confronts man's self-understanding.[19] The basis of this integrated vision of history is to be found in the principle that "there is no such thing as uninterpreted events in history" since he who selects interprets.[20] In other words the notion of pure "scientific history" is quite unreal. It is only as something human, meaningful, and conditioned by personal attitudes that history becomes present. Even in the case of "scientific knowledge" whether in the social sciences or in the natural sciences, the so-called "objective" is always tinged by a tissue of personal priorities, appropriations and interpretations. Pannenberg sums up this unified vision in the context of revelation by pointing out that history "is not composed of raw or so-called brute facts. As the history of man the history of salvation is always bound up with an understanding in hope and remembrance."[21] The same kind of unified outlook concerning the meaning of history can be found in the *Dogmatic Constitution on Divine Revelation* from the Second Vatican Council, which states explicitly that "the plan of Revelation is realised by deeds [events] and words [interpretation of events] having an inner unity".[22]

In addition, if this more unified vision of history is to yield fruit then it is important to situate the particular history under review in its proper socio-religious tradition. In the context of the historical Jesus this means situating the life of Jesus in the mainstream of Judaism. This in turn demands that we approach the history of Jesus from within a position of basic faith or more specifically basic Jewish faith. We can only search out the significance of the life of the historical Jesus from the background of basic Jewish faith. It would be impossible to fully appreciate the life of the historical Jesus from a neutral position outside faith. We must therefore presume the existence of some form of basic faith against which we investigate the historical life of Jesus.

It is important to keep in mind this background of basic faith in our next chapters when we come to map out the historical foundations of the Christ-Event. If we can do this then we will avoid on the one hand the extremes of the liberal lives of Jesus which tried to get back to the so-called pure facts, and on the other hand the stubborn scepticism of Bultmann and company who hold that it is impossible to go back behind the Christian faith picture of the gospels to the historical foundations of Christianity. Instead we will try to steer a middle course between these two extremes by confronting the historical reality of the man Jesus as it gradually and progressively unfolds itself upon the basic faith experience of the apostles.

Another significant point belonging to this emerging

consensus of biblical research within the context of the first layer of tradition is the existence of certain criteria for establishing authentic sayings of the historical Jesus. These criteria which are more or less universally accepted may be summarised as follows :

(a) Sayings that contain Aramaicisms reflect a Palestinian condition and therefore in all probability go back to the historical Jesus.

(b) When two or three different accounts of a particular incident are recorded the short form is to be preferred as more original. This criterion is based on the recognised tendency of authors to expand and explain.

(c) Traditions attributed to Jesus which are contrary to the developing traditions of the early Church are usually more authentic.

(d) Elements in the message of Jesus which make a break with the accepted traditions and customs of Judaism often point towards authenticity.

(e) Sayings that reflect the faith, practice and situation of the post-Easter Church cannot always be attributed to Jesus.

(f) The multiple attestations of certain words and deeds usually have a historical basis.[23]

The coordination of these criteria and their application to the gospel material is now regarded as a useful aid for going back to the historical life of Jesus. It must be pointed out however that these criteria do have their limitations.[24] They should not be used as individual criteria in isolation from each other. Instead they have a cross-checking, supporting interdependence which yields a type of cumulative result.

A final element within this emerging consensus of biblical research into the gospel traditions is the recognition of three distinct cultural strands that have influenced the formation of the gospel material. There is first of all the cultural strand of Palestinian Judaism. This would represent the original context in which Jesus was first understood and would therefore be determined by the theological Hebrew heritage of the Old Testament and inter-Testamental Judaism. Then there is the second cultural strand of Hellenistic Judaism. This would give rise to an understanding of Jesus shaped by the theological vision resulting from the transition of Jews into the Hellenistic world and their translation of the Hebrew scriptures into the Old Testament Greek Septuagint version. Lastly, there is the directly Hellenistic strand. This would produce an understanding of Jesus influenced by categories taken from the Greek-speaking gentiles who were converted to Christianity.[25]

On the other hand these cultural strands should not be taken as totally distinct and different in themselves. In fact there was, from the beginning, a certain Palestinian pluralism in existence during the life of Jesus which would already have included some elements of Hellenisation. To this extent the cultural strands should be used more as tools for analysing the different developments in the gospels rather than exact replicas of extrinsically distinct christologies.

It is only in the light of this review of the old-new-ongoing quest of the historical Jesus and this analysis of the various elements within the emerging consensus concerning biblical research that one can begin to appreciate the problem of the historical Jesus which lies at the foundations of the Christ-Event. This problem of the historical Jesus includes questions like : What kind of a picture of the historical Jesus does biblical research yield by going back behind the gospels? How does this historical life of Jesus give rise to the Christ-Event? In what way does the universal significance of the Christ-Event emerge from scripture and tradition? What role does the historical Jesus play within christology? And finally: What is the relationship between the Jesus of history and the Christ of faith? These questions cannot be answered all at once. They can only be approached systematically, step by step, each in its own turn and in its proper place.

3 Rediscovering the historical Jesus

We must now apply the various elements of the emerging consensus in biblical research to the New Testament picture of Jesus as the Christ and the Risen Lord. This will involve peeling away the different layers of tradition in the gospels that surround the Christ-Event. In particular it will necessitate taking into consideration the formative influence that the Resurrection and Pentecostal experiences had upon the apostles in understanding the life of the historical Jesus. To achieve this, special care will have to be taken not to read the gospels through the spectacles of the early Church, Nicea or Chalcedon. Instead the historical Jesus must be relocated within the particular socio-religious traditions of his day and not those of subsequent centuries. In so far as this is possible we will try to get back to the type of original impact that Jesus had upon those around him.

In doing this our primary purpose will be to quarry out of the gospels through the aid of biblical research a hard historical nucleus of meaningfully interpreted facts about Jesus of Nazareth that will serve as a historical minimum for understanding the recognition of Jesus as the Christ and Lord. In addition, this historical minimum will also provide us with a basic starting point in our low-ascending christology.

An historical minimum in the life of Jesus

Jesus appears first and foremost as a man among men. If there is one thing that comes across loud and clear in the New Testament it is the fact that Jesus was *a* man, being "taken from among men" (*Heb 5:1*), "born of a woman" (*Gal 4:4*), "belonging to the seed of David" (*2 Tim 2:8*), and "sharing the same flesh and blood as the rest of mankind" (*Heb 2:14*). As a man among men he appeared externally to those around him in exactly the same way as any other human individual appears. He experienced fatigue, hunger, disappointment, loneliness and the usual limitations in knowledge that belong to the human condition. Luke reminds us vividly that he "increased in wisdom and stature and in favour with God and men" (*Lk 2:52*). Matthew has Jesus openly declare his ignorance about the end of time. "But of that day and hour no one knows, not even the angels in heaven, nor the Son but the Father only" (*Mt 24:36*).[1]

Jesus is seen as a Rabbi (*Jn 1:38; 3:2; Mt 23:8*). He proclaims the divine law, he teaches in the synagogues, he gathers disciples, he debates with the other scribes, and he appeals to the authority of the scriptures. Yet he differs from the traditional type of rabbi in that he teaches not only in the synagogues but also in the open fields and on the lake shores. His followers are among those whom an official rabbi would avoid, such as women and children, tax collectors, and sinners.[2]

Jesus is understood as a prophet[3] within the long line of prophets that had gone before him. He refers to himself as a prophet when he points out that "no prophet is ever accepted in his own country" (*Lk 4:24*). Further, he likens his rejection to that of other prophets (*Mt 23:37*) and indicates in reference to himself that it ill becomes a prophet to die outside Jerusalem (*Lk 13:33*). In the eyes of those around him he clearly comes across as a prophet. This is the view of others which the disciples reported to him at Caesarea Philippi (*Mk 8:28*). It was the common opinion which came to Herod about Jesus (*Mk 6:15*). It was the reaction of the crowds to his entry into Jerusalem. They exclaimed: "This is the prophet Jesus from Nazareth" (*Mt 21:11*). Many of his mighty works marked him out as a prophet: "a great *prophet* has arisen among us" (*Lk 7:16*).

A prophet in those days was usually understood as an authoritative messenger and spokesman of God. As such the prophet is one who is "called" and "sent" by God (*Is 6:8; Jer 1:7; Ez 2:3; Ex 3:4-22*) and therefore one who speaks in the name of God so that his word becomes the Word of God (*Is 6:6; Ez 9:1-4*). To receive a prophet is to receive God. Thus we find the crowds referring to Jesus as a prophet and in the same breath claiming: "God has visited his people" (*Lk 6:16*). It is within the context of these prophetic qualities that much of the life-style of Jesus seems to be structured. A good example of this can be found in the baptism of Jesus. The theophany accompanying this event and the going forth with a mission is very characteristic of the prophetic call.

In particular Jesus is the prophet who proclaims the Kingdom of God. The first three gospels summarise the mission of Jesus in terms of preaching the Kingdom of God (*Mk 1:15; Mt 4:23; Lk 4:43*). Most of the miracles and the parables are centred around it. As such the Kingdom of God is preached as an imminent reality and this imminence has a double dimension to it. On the one hand the Kingdom of God is preached as a present reality breaking in upon the world in and through the mission of Jesus. On the other hand it is a future reality awaiting final fulfilment.

This rich Jewish concept of the Kingdom of God stood for the beginning of the messianic era in which a new order of things would be inaugurated. This new order was symbolised in a variety of ways. It included such things as a cosmic renewal, a return to some paradisial condition, a time of peace and prosperity, in which the wolf lives with the lamb and the panther lies down with the kid (*Is 11:6*). Most of all it was a state of affairs in which· the power and presence of Yahweh would reign in the midst of his people. For the Jew it was the messiah that would be instrumental in setting up this new order. Within this vision the emphasis was on the new state of things rather than on the figure of the messiah.

During the time of Jesus these messianic hopes and expectations had become distorted and literalised. It was a political kingdom that the Jews now looked forward to in the hope of achieving the material sovereignty of Israel over the Romans through a military triumph. As a result the role of the messiah had come to be understood in political terms. It was within this climate of thought that Jesus preached the Kingdom of God, trying to wean his audiences away from a materialistic understanding of his message to a more socio-spiritual vision. Thus much of the preaching of Jesus on the Kingdom of God is presented in parable form as a means of effecting a gradual change in his listeners. Furthermore it is this background of distortion concerning the Kingdom of God and the messianic era that explains why Jesus is so reluctant to be associated with the figure of the messiah during his public ministry.

Within the context of the Kingdom of God Jesus issues a radical call to repentance and faith. "The Kingdom of God is at hand. Repent, and believe in the Gospel" (*Mk 1:15*). This call is something that goes to the very roots of man's being, demanding a fundamental change of heart (metanoia). It requires a radical response bringing about a critical decision in the life of the individual in terms of rejection or acceptance. "No servant can serve two masters . . ." (*Lk 16:13*). "He who is not with me is against me, and he who does not gather with me scatters" (*Lk 11:23*). There is no zone of neutrality here; it is all or nothing. Arising out of this call is a special invitation to discipleship which reaches a climax in the selection of the twelve apostles whom he instructs and sets aside for a definite purpose.[4]

Jesus appears as a miracle worker alongside the many others who also worked miracles in those days. The primary difference between Jesus as a miracle worker and his contemporaries is the fact that in the majority of cases he worked miracles as a response to the presence of faith in his own person (*Mk 10:46-52*). In some cases the climactic point is not the miracle but Jesus's word of praise about the faith of the petitioner (*Mt 8:13; 9:22,29; 15:28*). The primary purpose of the miracles was to symbolise the inbreaking of the Kingdom of God and the defeat of evil forces. The actual conquest of such forces of evil was predicted as the time of salvation (*Is 29:18; 35:5f*). In this sense the miracles, or better, "the acts of power" (*dynamis*), or "signs" (*semeion*) and "works" (*ergon*) as they are called by the synoptics and John respectively are best understood as a symbolic dimension of the mission of Jesus in which and through which the power and presence of Yahweh was being made manifest.[5]

Jesus emerges as one speaking with great authority (*Mk 1:22; Jn 7:46*). His claim to special authority is brought out forcefully in the Sermon on the Mount, especially in such phrases as "You have heard that it was said to the men of old . . . but I say to you" (*Mt 5:21-22*). His use of the phrase "Amen" to introduce his teaching is also indicative of the authority emanating from him.[6] The normal practice for a Jew was to conclude his prayer to God with the expression "Amen" in the hope that God would act on it whereas Jesus prefaces his words with an "Amen", thereby indicating a prior rapport with God which is now communicated through his words. Further his claim to authority is accentuated by the contrast he makes between himself and Moses, between his teaching and the teaching of the Mosaic law which for the Jew had become identified with the will of God. In addition his power over the Sabbath (*Mt 12:1-8*) and the performance of exorcisms also signal his authority (*Mk 1:27; Lk 4:36*).

In particular his claim to forgive sins highlights this authority (*Mk 2:10; Mt 9:6; Lk 5:24*). Within Judaism the sinner was regarded as one who had cut himself off from the covenant relationship with Yahweh and who was therefore to be avoided. In contrast to this, here was a prophet stepping forward claiming to heal the breach and re-establish the broken relationship with God and one's fellow men. Not only that but Jesus seems to have gone out of his way to befriend the sinner, setting up a new type of table fellowship. This table fellowship initiated by Jesus became a symbol realising the present table fellowship "of the Kingdom" and anticipating the future table fellowship "in the Kingdom". To consort with outcasts in this way in the name of the kingdom of God which stood at the centre of Jewish hope was to offend the Jews of the day.[7]

Jesus is experienced as one preaching and promising salvation. On several occasions he employs various symbols to indicate the salvific nature of his mission. He describes himself as a physician for the sick (*Mk 2:17*), and as a shepherd who cares for his flock (*Mk 14:27f; Jn 10*). An intrinsic component of this salvation which he preached was the promotion of a radical ethic of interiority which transcended the external letter of the Jewish law (*Mt 23:1-26*). This ethic of interiority is summed up in the great commandment of universal love of God and of neighbour.[8]

Most of all Jesus appears as one who dares to assume a unique personal closeness to the monotheistic God of Judaism. This allows him to address Yahweh as Abba— Father (*Mk 14:36*). The personal address of Yahweh as "My Father" is something that stands out as uniquely original to Jesus in the literature of Palestinian Judaism.[9] Stemming from this close relationship with God as Father is the underlying presence of a radically theocentric outlook in the life of the historical Jesus. This theocentric outlook shows itself on several different levels throughout the life of Jesus. For one thing it is the Kingdom of God that Jesus preaches and not himself. Further there is the presence of a filial relationship towards God as Father. Within this relationship there is an equally strong sense of personal and vocational obedience to God as Father in his work. Lastly this theocentric quality can be seen in the presence of prayer as a God-directed activity which takes place throughout the ministry of Jesus, but especially at key moments in his life (*Lk 3:21; 6:12; 9:28*).

One of the most significant factors about the life of the historical Jesus is the fact that his preaching and teaching is delivered from within an apocalyptic framework.[10] This does not mean that we should see or think of Jesus as an apocalyptist indulging in imaginative projections about the future. It does however suggest that we can only fully appreciate the activity of Jesus against the historical background of apocalyptic expectation. This should be clear in view of the fact that the Kingdom of God concept which is so central to the whole life of Jesus bears the stamp of apocalyptic origins.[11] Further it is possible to detect within the words and deeds of the historical Jesus an underlying tension between present and future, between promise and fulfilment. This can be seen in his preaching of the Kingdom of God, his claim to authority, and his promise of salvation, each of which requires further fulfilment and future realisation. This type of tension within the preaching of Jesus corresponds most closely to the apocalyptic outlook which also contains a similar pull between promise and fulfilment by grasping future events before they actually occur, and thereby requiring their future confirmation through the course of history.[12]

Within this context of an apocalyptic framework the most comprehensive category in which to understand the life of the historical Jesus is to see him as "the eschatological prophet". It is this category that was probably most real for the contemporaries of Jesus.[13] We have already seen that it was quite clear that Jesus came across as a prophet within the long line of prophets that had gone before him. During the time preceding Jesus there had been an absence of prophets within Judaism. Out of this

absence grew the presence of a hope for the coming of
a final or eschatological prophet who would rise up in
the last days. This hope of an eschatological prophet was
understood in terms of a return of a Moses-like prophet
(*Deut 18:15-19*) or the reappearance of Elijah (*Mal 4:5 ff*).
Initially it is John the Baptist who is hailed as Elijah
(*Mk 6:15; Jn 1:21*). However, John later denies that he
is Elijah and suggests that it is Jesus who is the real Elijah,
the man who will baptise with the Holy Spirit and with fire
(*Mk 3:11*). Further, there is the evidence that the contemporaries of Jesus also saw him as Elijah (*Mk 6:14ff; 8:28*).
To this extent it seems most reasonable and historically
reliable to hold that Jesus at this stage of his life would
have been seen as the eschatological prophet. Not only
that, but this category seems to sum up most comprehensively the overall thrust that the ministry of Jesus would
have had upon his followers at this point in his life. As
eschatological prophet he announced the end of time, he
proclaimed the Kingdom of God, he performed eschatological signs (miracles and exorcisms) and he heralded the
advent of salvation.[14]

The closing stages in the life of Jesus

The underlying impact of these different words and deeds
must have been one that singled out the historical Jesus
as a unique and extraordinary figure within the history
of Judaism. As such the ministry of Jesus is extremely
suggestive and heavily laden with all kinds of messianic
and apocalyptic implications. Yet a certain ambiguity and
incompleteness hangs over these words and deeds of Jesus.
This ambiguity and incompleteness is sharpened by the
underlying tension between the present and the future,
between promise and fulfilment.[15] To this extent the meaning and significance of the life of the historical Jesus requires
further clarification, confirmation, and fulfilment. At this

stage therefore there can be no question of the apostles
fully understanding Jesus as the Christ and Lord. Instead
the response of the apostles to Jesus is best understood in
terms of a strong basic Jewish faith that had become Jesus-
centred in the hope that he would be the one to restore
the Kingdom of Israel (*Lk 24:21*). This should be clear
when one remembers that the fate and destiny of Jesus
still remain quite uncertain and obscure. To complete our
outline of the historical minimum required for understanding the life of the historical Jesus we must now turn to
the closing stages of his earthly life.

The death of Jesus must never be isolated from the
historical life that preceded it. Instead it should be seen
as the culminating point of the extraordinary words and
deeds of Jesus which we have been examining. The death
of Jesus was something that happened to him as an
intrinsic consequence of his earlier life; it was not something
that he went out of his way to choose in some inhuman
manner.

The words and deeds of the historical Jesus brought
him into direct conflict with the official leaders of Judaism.
Here was a prophet setting himself up above the authority
of Moses, claiming to forgive sin, initiating a new form
of table fellowship between God and man, promising
salvation, and criticising the established religious *status
quo*. These extravagant claims were too much for the hard-
hearted officials of Judaism; they were daring in the
extreme. "This is why the Jews sought all the more to
kill him because he not only broke the Sabbath but also
called God his Father" (*Jn 5:18*). The rejection of Jesus
was inevitable for any Jew who was loyal to the law since
in those days the authority of the law had become identified
with the authority of Israel's God. Thus we find Jesus being
accused of blasphemy (*Mk 2:7; 14:64*). This accusation
could not be one of blasphemy in the narrow sense since
Jesus did not revile the name of God (*Lev 24:10-23*), or
pronounce the ineffable name of Yahweh. Rather it was

blasphemy in the sense that Jesus appeared to be assuming unto himself certain divine prerogatives and power.

During his public life Jesus must have reckoned with the possibility of death. The destiny of previous prophets was surely an indication of the way his own life was likely to be determined. Further we find Jesus referring to "the killing of prophets and the stoning of those who are sent to you" (*Lk 13:34*), which had gone on before him. The parable of the wicked husbandmen also alludes to the same kind of thing (*Mk 12:1-12*). The fate of John the Baptist at the hands of Herod must have heightened his own awareness of what lay in store for him, especially since he had aligned so much of his own ministry with that of John the Baptist (*Mt 11:11-14; 21:32; Mk 11:27ff*). In addition many of the charges levelled against him such as the casting out of demons with the help of Beelzebub (*Mt 12:24*), being a false prophet, deliberately breaking the Sabbath, and that he blasphemed were punishable by stoning or by death.[16]

There can be no doubt that the journey up to Jerusalem by Jesus was a very significant, deliberate and conscious decision. It was significant in that for every Jew, as indeed for Jesus, Jerusalem was not only the capital but the place associated with the destiny of Israel (*Lk 19:11*). It was deliberate because at that time huge masses of people would be gathered in the city to celebrate the liberation of the people from Egypt and therefore messianic and apocalyptic expectations would be reawakened. It was a conscious act in that Jesus would have realised that the opposition between his mission and the political-religious leaders of the day was steadily growing.[17] Indeed it was the incident in the temple in Jerusalem that brought this opposition to a head when Jesus drove out those who were buying and selling in the house of God (*Mk 11:15-17*). "And the chief priests and scribes sought a way to destroy him; for they feared him; because all the multitude was astonished at his teaching" (*Mk 11:18*). In all probability this incident was followed historically by the arrest, the trial, and the execution, the details of which are extremely difficult to disentangle from a critical point of view. Because of this latter problem it is also difficult to decide who was ultimately responsible, Jews or Romans, for the death of Jesus. There can be no question that as time went on it became expedient both politically and religiously that Jesus should be done away with. However, the political expediency would seem to be something that was derived from the religious disturbance that Jesus was causing. To this extent the execution of Jesus would appear to have been both religiously inspired and politically opportune.[18]

The decision to go up to Jerusalem therefore was a turning point in the life of the historical Jesus. It marked his departure from the Galilean ministry and his explicit refusal to accept the way of a political messiah. In spite of this his disciples seemed to pin their hope on a triumphant appearance of the Kingdom as a result of this journey (Lk 19:11; 24:21). No matter how distorted, this expectation concerning the Kingdom must have had its roots and inspiration in the unfolding consciousness of Jesus himself. The impending prospect of death arising out of the mounting opposition now appears as the only way in which the truth of his words and deeds will emerge. The only avenue left for the realisation of God's Kingdom on earth is in and through the awesome reality of death itself. To this extent death for Jesus appears to be God-willed, taking on a divine necessity vis-à-vis the realisation of his mission. That death could assume such a positive significance is something that could have emerged from Jesus's direct or indirect acquaintance with the servant songs of Isaiah.[19] In addition late Jewish apocalyptic thinking seemed to attach positive value to the death of the martyrs as preparatory to the messianic period of the end time (Dan 11:38).

In this way an awareness of death as the instrument for the realisation of God's purpose and Kingdom would have taken place during the final stages of the earthly life of Jesus. This type of thinking seems to loom large during the Last Supper when Jesus says: "Truly, I tell you, I shall not drink again of the fruit of the vine until that day when I drink it anew in the Kingdom of God" (*Mk 14:25*). Further, Jesus seems to associate the Last Supper with his death as bound up with the realisation of God's plan. As such the Last Supper at this stage is best understood as a prophetic act taking place within the apocalyptic setting of the rest of the life of Jesus.

For the disciples of Jesus his death on the cross spelt failure. It was the supreme crisis-moment for his followers. Their hopes had been dashed and their faith shattered. A deep sense of loss, disappointment, and exasperation ensued. The cross was indeed both a stumbling block and a sheer scandal.

4 The resurrection: a survey of the evidence

Having examined critically the life of the historical Jesus we can move on to the mystery of the resurrection. To try to understand the historical foundations of the Christ-Event without taking into consideration the resurrection is to do violence to the plan of God's revelation in Jesus of Nazareth. For too long the resurrection has been presented merely as a motive for understanding Jesus whereas it is both motive and object of faith in the Christ-Event.

The primary context for understanding the mystery of the resurrection is the historical life of Jesus. As already noted the preaching and teaching of the historical Jesus evoked a faith response in terms of strong Jewish faith that had become Jesus-centred. It is against this background that we must now approach the resurrection. Without this prior faith disposition in the life of the historical Jesus as induced by his suggestive words and deeds the resurrection will appear as a strange and inexplicable phenomenon. The story of Dives and Lazarus (*Lk 16:19-31*) underlines this point. Dives, from Hades, wants to warn his brothers against falling into the same place of torment. He asks Abraham to send Lazarus to his brothers. Abraham replies, "If they do not hear Moses and the prophets, neither will they be convinced if someone should rise from the dead" (*Lk 16:31*). In the same way unless we have followed the different words and deeds of the historical Jesus in faith we shall not be able to understand the resurrection. In other words the resurrection must not be presented as some extraordinary event which forces faith. Instead it should appear

44

as the realisation and crystallisation of the different dimensions implicit in the preaching and teaching of Jesus.

Following the lines of the last chapter our examination
of the resurrection will be based on biblical and historical
research. Certain theological observations, however, will
have to be made as we go along in virtue of the fact that
the resurrection narratives have been written up from a
highly theological point of view.

It is as well also at this stage to point out that no one
saw the resurrection. The only evidence we have for the
resurrection is the appearances and the empty tomb. The
resurrection itself is an act of God upon Jesus. As an act
of God, it could not have been seen. The only mode of
access that we have to an act of God is in and through
the effects or results of that particular act of God. In the
case of the resurrection these effects are the appearances,
the empty tomb and the reality of Christianity itself.

As a starting point to our examination of the evidence
we can say from a historical point of view that "something
happened" after the death of Jesus, irrespective of how
we describe this "something". This would seem to be the
minimum necessary for any reasonable discussion of the
resurrection. It is a minimum that should be acceptable
to most historians as a basic point of departure.

The Pauline evidence

The most important evidence for the resurrection is to be
found in *1 Cor 15:3-8* which may be laid out schematically
as follows :

> For I delivered to you as of first importance what I
> also received
> that Christ died for our sins in accordance with the
> Scriptures
> that he was buried
> that he was raised on the third day in accordance with
> the Scriptures

that he appeared to Cephas
then to the twelve
then . . . to more than five hundred
most of whom are still alive,
though some have fallen asleep.
Then he appeared to James
to all the apostles
last of all as to one untimely born
he appeared also to me.

These verses are important for a variety of reasons.[1] For one thing Paul is passing on a tradition which he himself received (v. 3). This is quite clear from the language he uses. Words like "sins" (*hamartion*), "appeared" (*ophthe*), and "the twelve" (*dodeka*) do not normally belong to Paul's vocabulary. Instead, Paul normally uses "sin" (*hamartia*) in the singular, "revealed" (*apocalypsis*) in regard to the resurrection, and "apostles" (*apostoloi*) in preference to "the twelve". Further, this tradition can be traced back to existence within less than ten years of the events it reports. Although the letter to the Corinthians was written around the year 56–57 A.D., the only time Paul could have received this formulated tradition would have been during his visit to Jerusalem (*Gal 1:18*) in the year 38 A.D. or more probably during his conversion in the year 35 A.D. Lastly, the construction of these verses reflects an Aramaic[2] or Hebrew[3] background which strengthens our suggestion of a very early tradition. In all probability we are dealing with verses that were originally drawn up as catechetical or liturgical formulae very early in the life of the Church.

Our analysis of this formula must restrict itself to the more important verses. The first among these is that "he was raised on the third day in accordance with the Scriptures" (v. 3). The language of "rising" or "being raised up" is taken from the daily experience of awakening

or rising up from sleep in the morning.[4] When used in an
apocalyptic context, as it is here by Paul,[5] it is intended
to indicate the transition from one mode of existence into
a new mode of existence (*Is 26:19; Dan 12:3; Enoch
92:32*). The exact nature of this transition is a matter of
dispute within late Judaism.[6]

When one turns to the rest of chapter fifteen of
Corinthians, however, which is really a commentary on
this early formula, one gets some light on the nature of
the transition involved in the resurrection of Jesus. Although
most of Paul's commentary is taken up with the resurrection of the Christian it can be presumed that his reflections
are based on his understanding of the resurrection of Jesus.
Commenting on the body of those who will rise Paul insists
that it will not be the same physical body:

What is sown is perishable, what is raised is
imperishable.
It is sown in dishonour, it is raised in glory.
It is sown in weakness, it is raised in power.
It is sown a physical body, it is raised a spiritual body.
If there is a physical body there is also a spiritual body
(*1 Cor 15:42-44;* cf. also *vv. 51:53*).

Of particular interest here is the contrast Paul makes
between a physical body (*soma psuchikos*) of this life and
the spiritual body (*soma pneumatikos*) of the hereafter.[7]
Within this contrast the underlying reality which remains
is that of man's body/personality (*soma*) which is the
enduring corporeal quality of man's inner being and which
is the originating source of his ability to relate. In this life
the somatic reality of man's personality relates to the world
around him, in and through the perishable and opaque
medium of the flesh (*sarx*). In the next life this underlying
corporeal character of man's being as fleshified is transformed through the resurrection by being filled with the
transparency of the spirit; in this case the spirit of God.[8]

It becomes quite clear that this particular antithesis

as well as the others in verses *42-43* indicate that the transition involved in resurrection is one of transformation. Paul describes this transformation through the image of sowing a seed (*v. 37*). One sows a seed and what comes up in continuity is a radically transformed stalk of wheat. It is in this sense that Paul can refer to the risen Jesus as "the first fruits of those who have fallen asleep" (*1 Cor 15:20*) and so highlight the element of transformation involved in the transition that takes place in resurrection.

The expression "he was raised" means therefore that the resurrection of Jesus from the dead involved a transition and that this transition was one of personal transformation. This element of transformation points towards the metaphorical character of resurrection language. The image of rising up in the morning is used to describe something of which no man has direct experience in this life, namely the transition and transformation that takes place in Jesus through death. The resurrection of Jesus from the dead therefore must not be understood literally in terms of a physical resuscitation or merely as a restoration to life of his old earthly body in the way that Lazarus was brought back temporarily to life. Rather the resurrection of Jesus involves something much more than this; something that can only be described symbolically in terms of change, difference, newness, and transformation.[9]

The next important phrase is that "he appeared" (*v. 5*). The Greek verb used for "he appeared" (*ophthe*) is notoriously difficult to understand and to translate accurately. The best English equivalent is that "he was seen" or better "he was made manifest". In the light of its use in the Greek Old Testament to describe divine epiphanies (*Gen 12:7; Ex 3:2f*) this verb implies at least two important points. On the one hand it suggests a becoming visible of that which belongs to the world of invisibility.[10] This becoming visible, this making manifest, depends primarily on that which makes itself known.[11] The initiative comes from the reality manifesting itself in a way that supposes the presence of some external phenomenon coming in on the recipient from the outside. To this extent the origin of the appearances would seem to depend on a reality coming in from the outside rather than on the subjective dispositions of those who claim to have experienced the risen Jesus. Indeed the use of this expression "he appeared" would seem to be "a protest . . . against attempts to divest the Easter Event of its objective character".[12] On the other hand the verb "he appeared" also suggests some form of revelatory experience for those who were the recipients of this manifestation. This would involve the subjective dispositions of those who received the revelation whereby they now experience and understand Jesus in a new way. This revelatory experience is probably best understood in terms of a visual experience giving rise to new insight.

The final important part of this early tradition is the actual listing of various eye-witnesses, many of whom Paul assures us are still around so that they can be checked out if necessary (v. 6). This enumeration of different witnesses seems to point once more towards some form of real experience over and above a purely internal experience. It would be difficult from a purely psychological point of view to synchronise such a wide range of individual experiences unless there was some real basis in reality behind them. Furthermore references to concrete individual people who actually experience the appearances of the risen Jesus introduce a certain historical character into Paul's evidence. The appearances occurred to certain people : Cephas, the Twelve, and Five Hundred; at a certain time (in the middle of the first century as distinct from the twentieth century); in a certain place (Palestine as distinct from Ireland). These basic facts would seem to allow us to talk about the appearances as historical from the point of view of those who encountered the risen Jesus.

Having raised the historical question at this juncture it should be pointed out that the resurrection event as distinct from the appearances is unhistorical or better trans-historical. It is trans-historical in the sense that it refers to an "event" that took place on the other side of death which lies outside the conditions of space and time. Similarly the reality resulting from this event, namely the reality of the risen Jesus, is also a trans-historical reality in that it belongs to the end of history existing within the new (eschatological) era. To say this, however, in no way invalidates the historicity of the appearances; it merely safeguards the other-worldly new reality of the risen Jesus.

This brief analysis of the earliest tradition about the resurrection of Jesus enables us to make some elementary remarks about the "something" that happened after the death of Jesus. This "something" is grounded in a real experience of actual appearances. This real experience is interpreted in terms of resurrection. The language of resurrection is metaphorical, describing the transition and personal transformation that occurred to Jesus after his death. This personal transformation manifests itself through appearances which were real, historical, and revelatory experiences.

The evangelists

We can now move on to examine the gospel reports about the resurrection of Jesus. It is important to remember that the gospels were only finally drawn up some 33-65 years after the death of Jesus. This means in effect that there is a considerable distance between the gospels and the original events which they describe. Within the gospels there are reports about the appearances of Jesus and about the finding of an empty tomb. We shall deal with these separately.

Concerning the appearances there is a rich variety of different accounts; a variety which develops certain inconsistencies when it comes to specific details. Broadly speaking there are six distinguishable accounts of the appearances which can be conveniently divided into two different traditions: those concerned with the appearances of Jesus in Galilee (*Mt 28; Jn 21; Mk 16:1-8* by implication) and those concerned with the appearances to the eleven in Jerusalem (*Lk 24; Jn 20; Mk 16:9-20*). Neither tradition seems to make allowance for, or show any awareness of, the existence of the other tradition.[13] Numerous attempts have been made to overcome these discrepancies through a process of harmonisation. This is now regarded by most commentators[14] as an unprofitable if not an impossible exercise.

A more realistic approach is to accept the discrepancies as inevitable in view of the lateness of the reports and the nature of the events they are trying to relate. It is a fact of life that reporters and witnesses are notorious for providing conflicting evidence, especially when it concerns something new and different. In addition, since we have different authors, writing to different communities, with different purposes, at different times, there are bound to be differences when it comes to detail. Furthermore, it is generally accepted that the gospel narratives on the resurrection contain a high degree of development and dramatisation which has been determined by theological and apologetical interests.[15] Yet in spite of these elements which have created discrepancies in detail it must be acknowledged that the overriding factor common to all accounts is the given fact that Jesus of Nazareth is reported as having appeared to his disciples after his death. The substance and function of these dramatised and divergent accounts is the same fundamental experience that Jesus is risen and alive. Furthermore it is possible to detect the presence of a fairly common pattern[16] running through this fundamental experience as described in the gospel accounts which may be summarised as follows:

(a) The circumstances of the appearances are the same in that the followers of Jesus are despondent and disappointed. "But we had hoped that he was the one to redeem Israel" (*Lk 24:21;* cf. also *Jn 20:19*).

(b) The initiative for the appearances comes from Jesus. "Jesus came and stood among them" (*Jn 20:19;* cf. also *Lk 24:15; Mt 28:9, 18*).

(c) There is some form of greeting from Jesus. "Peace be with you" (*Jn 20:19;* cf. also *Mt 28:9*).

(d) A moment of recognition follows. "It is the Lord" (*Jn 21:7;* cf. also *Jn 20:20; Mt 28:9, 17*).

(e) A word of command from Jesus concludes the experience. "Go therefore and make disciples" (*Mt 28:19;* cf. also *Mt 28:10; Jn 20:21; Jn 21:15ff; Lk 24:26ff*).

The climactic point within this recurring pattern is "the moment of recognition". An experience of recognition normally involves the bringing together in association a likeness from the past with a change in the present as the result of an encounter with some extramental reality. In the gospels this experience of recognition combines a situation of fear and doubt (*Mt 28:10, 17*) which gradually gives way to reassurance (*Jn 21:7*). These elements of hesitancy and reassurance point towards the presence of "likeness" and "change" in the reality of the risen Jesus who is recognised. It is this tension between "sameness" and "difference" arising out of the reality experienced that lies behind the contrasting descriptions of the appearances.

The element of sameness is brought out in the stress on corporeal continuity that exists between the crucified Jesus and the risen Jesus. This stress can be seen in the dramatised descriptions of "touching" (*Jn 20:27*), "eating" (*Lk 24:41-43*) and "speaking" (*Jn 21:15ff*). These descriptions tend to physicalise the apostles' experience with the risen Jesus in a way that reflects more the artistry of effective narration than the literal description of what really happened.[17] The purpose behind these artistic literary forms and editorialised narratives is manifold. For one thing it is to drive home the underlying identity and continuity between the historical Jesus and the risen Jesus. It is also to highlight the realness of the corporeal resurrection of Jesus as distinct from a purely spiritual resurrection which would have been the way the Greek mind, with its philosophy of the immortality of the soul, would have tended to understand resurrection.[18] In addition it is to overcome the presence of gnostic and docetic interpretations of Jesus that were beginning to appear in the second half of the first century.

On the other hand, however, these references to sameness are counterbalanced by an equally strong emphasis on "difference". This emphasis underlines the discontinuity or better the transformation that exists between the earthly Jesus and the risen Jesus. This can be found in those accounts where we are told that they did not recognise him as he stood before them (*Lk 24:16; Jn 20:14; 21:4*) and that some even doubted that it was he (*Mt 28:17; Lk 24:41*). Further we are informed that the risen Jesus "comes" (*Lk 24:31; Jn 20:19, 26*) and "goes" in a way that no earthly body does, thus indicating the otherness of the risen Jesus who is no longer bound by space and time.[19] Mark is quite explicit in this regard, pointing out that "he appeared in another form" (*Mk 16:12*). The importance of this emphasis is that it guards against understanding the resurrection as a mere return to earthly existence and focuses upon the change that has taken place in the resurrection of Jesus from the dead. These references to change re-echo Paul's teaching on the element of transformation. In all probability it was such references to change and to transformation that constituted the earliest emphasis of the infant Church.

The gospel accounts therefore of the appearances all agree that the apostles had an experience of Jesus as risen and alive. This experience is quite different from the type of experience the apostles had of Jesus before his death. Yet in spite of the difference the gospels are insistent that it is the same Jesus that the apostles had known before his death and who is now present to them in a new way. Throughout the gospel reports there is a continual emphasis on this dual dimension of continuity and change within the resurrection experiences. In a word, there is an underlying identity within transformation between the historical Jesus and the risen Jesus.

Within the context of this understanding of the appearances of Jesus we can now turn to the question of the empty tomb. Like the appearances, the empty tomb accounts are dotted with inconsistencies[20] and embellishments, the details of which need not delay us. The first and probably the most important point to note is that the empty tomb tradition in itself is an ambiguous piece of evidence. The immediate reaction of the women to the discovery of the empty tomb brings this out. Mark tells us unashamedly that the women "went out and fled from the tomb; for trembling and astonishment had come upon them and they said nothing to anyone" (*Mk 16:8*). Luke is even more direct, pointing out that the report of the empty tomb by the women initially at least "seemed to them (the apostles) an idle tale and they did not believe them" (*Lk 24:11*). In itself therefore the fact of the empty tomb proves nothing. It simply raises questions like what happened, how did the tomb become empty, could there be a mistake, did someone perhaps steal the body? To this extent the story of the empty tomb is ambiguous; it invites the reader to make further enquiry.

This further enquiry leads to the question of the origins of the empty tomb tradition. Some have argued that it belongs to a "primitive pre-literary tradition".[21] Others have argued that it is a late tradition brought in for apologetic reasons. They would hasten to add, however, that lateness does not preclude historicity.[22] Lastly there are those who feel that the empty tomb is a non-historical legend.[23] This latter charge raises the more basic question of how reliable is the empty tomb tradition.

The nature of the evidence in the gospel concerning the empty tomb suggests a high degree of reliability. It is pointed out that the evidence of the women is particularly pressing since no author within that particular Jewish culture would have used female witnesses in a fabricated story. Women were simply not accepted at that time as witnesses. Further it is noted that the early Jewish controversies against the message of the resurrection all presupposed that the tomb was empty. The real question was: How did it become empty? Some said the disciples had stolen the body (*Mt 28:11-15; 27:64*); others that the gardener had taken it away (*Jn 20:13-15*) in order, as Tertullian (d. ca. 200 A.D.) colourfully adds, to keep his vegetables from being trampled on by visitors to the tomb! Probably the most convincing argument for the reliability of the empty tomb tradition is the simple fact that the transmission of this tradition would have been impossible if in fact the tomb lay intact.[24] For these reasons it is difficult to reduce the discovery of the empty tomb to the level of a non-historical legend.

What then was the significance of the empty tomb tradition? From a historical point of view it was an ambiguous piece of evidence open to any number of possible interpretations. In the light of the appearances however it assumes a positive significance pointing towards the complete conquest of death in the experience of Jesus as risen and alive. The primary resurrection experience however was the appearance of Jesus and not the empty tomb. In the light of this primary experience the empty tomb becomes a secondary negative piece of evidence for the resurrection corroborating the implications of the appearances. From a theological point of view it should be noted in passing that the object of Christian faith is the resurrection of Jesus and not the empty tomb as such.

The empty tomb as a fact of history like the empty tombs of the Egyptian Pharaohs, does not properly belong to the order of faith.[25] To this extent the empty tomb was more important in the early Church than it is for us today.[26] However from a theological point of view it may be taken as a negative sign of the continuity between the earthly Jesus and the risen Jesus as well as a safeguard against a docetic and gnostic understanding of the resurrection.

By way of conclusion we can say that the gospel accounts complement our earlier observations based on Paul about the "something" that happened after the death of Jesus. They do this by expanding and developing in dramatised form the implications of Paul's formula that Jesus was raised and appeared to the apostles. These implications amount to the fact that the apostles had a real historical and revelatory experience of Jesus as alive after his death and that this experience was mediated through the appearances, and interpreted in terms of personal resurrection from the dead.

What really happened?

In spite of our examination of the evidence for the resurrection many will still ask "But what really happened?" The temptation of course at this stage is to point out that a theological mystery like the resurrection is not something which is directly susceptible to empirical questions like: What really happened? While this may be true, and even then this type of statement requires careful explanation if it is to satisfy the enquiring mind, it is possible to go a little further if only through the *via negativa* in trying to meet this not untypical question in the minds of many today.

It should be clear from our investigation of the evidence that the apostles had a real experience of Jesus as alive after his death. It is the nature of this unique experience that must be analysed amongst other things in any attempt to explain what really happened. What kind of experience did the apostles have? Was it a subjective experience or did it have some basis in reality? If it had a basis in reality can we say anything about the nature of the reality they experienced?

Two extremes should be avoided in trying to answer these questions. The first of these is the view which says that the experience of the apostles was a purely subjective experience. Various explanations for this subjective view are put forward. For some the experience of the apostles was based on a subjective interior feeling that the cause of Jesus still goes on today.[27] For others, the life of the historical Jesus continued to inspire the apostles in spite of his death on the cross, so that it was this interior inspiration that gave rise to the resurrection narratives.[28] One way or the other there is a subjective internal experience in favour of the continuation of Jesus which is subsequently interpreted in the language of resurrection.[29]

Certain difficulties, however, arise with this type of subjectivist explanation of what really happened. First of all there is the underlying assumption in these subjectivist schools which excludes on *a priori* grounds the possibility of any real personal experience in view of the fact that this does not accord with modern man's experience. Arising out of this assumption is the presence of a prejudice which reads the New Testament evidence in a highly restrictive and reductionist manner. As a result the appearances are explained away as mere interpretative verbalisations of some subjective experience and the empty tomb tradition is automatically excluded as a late apologetic fiction. This way of reading the New Testament evidence is clearly quite incompatible with our above exposition of the appearances and the empty tomb. In particular it errs by placing itself outside the mainstream of basic Jewish faith which we regard as a necessary prerequisite for understanding the New Testament.

However, even if one were to pass over this particularly prejudiced and *a priori* approach to the New Testament evidence there still remain serious difficulties with the subjectivist school. How does one explain the source and origin of the appearances? What triggered off the particular subjective experience? Could pure subjectivity in experience give rise consistently to exactly the same type of basic interpretation among individuals who were quite different in background and mentality? What was the basis of interpreting this experience in the language of resurrection considering that the resurrection of a single individual was a novel and unexpected idea at that time?[30] Further, is there not a real difference in the New Testament itself between outward appearances as associated with the resurrection and internal visions as attributed to Peter and to Stephen in the *Acts of the Apostles,* especially in the language used to describe these different kinds of experiences? Most of all is it feasible to suggest that a subjective experience could suddenly produce a radical change and conversion in the lives of a small group of men whose faith had been shattered by the scandal of the cross and who are reported to have abandoned Jesus at Calvary and subsequently departed to their own ordinary lives? Is it conceivable on the strength of a subjective experience that these men can now suddenly begin to believe in the resurrection, go out to preach and witness to Jesus as risen, and develop a whole new understanding of life as centred around the resurrection, and then even be prepared to lay down their lives for the truth of this new understanding? In a word, how could the Church as we know it today with its particular body of doctrine and its message of hope have ever emerged and survived on the supposition of a purely subjective experience after the death of Jesus? If the resurrection of Jesus is based on a subjective experience of his followers, what then is the difference between the resurrection of Jesus and the resurrection, say, of

Beethoven through his music? If there is no substantial difference, then the elaborate doctrinal system such as the doctrine of the Holy Spirit, the reality of the Church, the presence of Christ in his Church and in its sacraments as well as the teaching on eternal life, all of which derive their inspiration from a real resurrection of Jesus, must be altered substantially if not done away with altogether. These, in brief, are some of the questions that the subjectivist school fail to answer adequately in their reductionist understanding of resurrection.

The other extreme to be avoided is that which we might loosely describe as the overly objectivist outlook on the appearances. Within this approach the appearances are presented like a reality "out there" to be experienced in the same way as any other historical reality "out there" might be experienced. Thus, the experience of the risen Jesus is reduced to the same type of experience as the apostles had of the earthly historical Jesus.

Like the subjectivist school this outlook has serious limitations. In general terms it over-simplifies the New Testament in a way that loses sight of the complex character and historical formation of the gospel material.[31] It does this by failing to allow for the dramatising development, the apologetical expansion, and the personal embroidering that goes into the telling and retelling of a new and different experience. In particular it literalises the dramatised descriptions of the appearance experiences. It fails to recognise the metaphorical character of resurrection language and the symbolic imagery used by Paul to describe the risen Jesus in terms of "a spiritual body" (1 Cor 15:44), the "first fruits" (1 Cor 15:20, 23), and "new creation" (2 Cor 5:17). Further, it neglects the newness of the experience associated with the risen Jesus. Lastly it ignores the incredulity and hesitancy of the apostles in accepting the resurrection of Jesus. Any reasonable assessment of what really happened after the death of Jesus must avoid these two extremes. Instead it must be attentive to the biblical evidence of past reports as well as trying to understand the meaning of resurrection within man's present experience.[32]

The first point to be remembered about the risen Jesus is that we are dealing with a reality that belongs to a new mode of being. This mode of being may be described theologically as an eschatological mode of existence. As such the reality of the risen Jesus is a transcendent reality and therefore it cannot be confined to ordinary everyday categories. On the other hand, however, this transcendent or other-worldly character of the risen Jesus is no less real simply because it is no longer limited by our conditions of space and time. On the contrary it could be argued that this transcendent mode of being belonging to the risen Jesus is all the more real because it is free from the historical limitations of life on this side of death.

It was this transcendent reality that the apostles experienced in and through the appearances of Jesus. Clearly the experience of this transcendent reality, though real and exterior to the apostles, cannot be reduced to the experience of just another object alongside other earthly objects. What kind of experience then did the apostles have?

The nearest parallel that we can find to describe the experience of the apostles is that of a "transforming experience". The image of a "transforming experience" is taken from a model of a person-to-person transforming experience. From time to time people do have experiences which deeply affect and influence their lives. One thinks for example of those rich experiences associated with special moments of fellowship, reconciliation, and solidarity. These kinds of experiences, in virtue of their gratuity, do in fact disarm and surprise, lift and renew, change and transform our lives. In a similar way the transcendent power of the risen Jesus was experienced by the apostles as a gracious fellowship, a personal reconciliation and a divine solidarity which did in fact disarm and surprise, lift and renew,

change and transform their lives. It is no mere coincidence
that many of the resurrection narratives are written up in
a language which is in fact trying to describe these kinds
of rich experiences. Not only that but the descriptions of
the transforming experience are developed into sacramental
encounters with the risen Jesus. For instance, the transforming experience of the risen Jesus is associated with
eucharistic fellowship (*Lk 24:13-25; Jn 21:1-14*), the forgiveness of sins (*Jn 20:21-23*), and the solidarity of his
Spirit (*Mt 28:16-20; Jn 20:22*). This association by the
apostles of their experience of the risen Jesus with the
sacraments is all the more significant for us today since
it highlights that the primary sources of our contact with
the risen Jesus are the sacraments.

Developing this interpersonal model we can say that
the transforming experience of the apostles by the risen
Jesus was an engaging and illuminating faith experience.
It was engaging in that the apostles found themselves
involved in a new relationship with the risen Jesus; it was
illuminating in that they were caught up in a new understanding of Jesus as risen. As such it was an experience
of a new, living, real and personal presence that allowed
them to affirm that God had raised Jesus from the dead.
This affirmation was not simply based on faith alone nor
was it an affirmation resulting exclusively from the appearances. The issue here cannot be reduced to either "faith
creates resurrection" or "resurrection creates faith". Rather,
these are intrinsically related dimensions of the same transforming experience. Those who had followed Jesus in faith
now come to recognise him in a different way as risen in
the light of their transforming experience of his new, real,
personal presence.

The advantage of drawing upon this model of a
person-to-person transforming experience is that it highlights the impossibility of adequately describing what really
happened after the death of Jesus. No amount of human
description can fully capture all the dimensions of a person-

to-person transforming experience; there is always a further dimension that cannot be grasped. In the same way the transforming experience of the apostles by the risen Jesus cannot be netted by human language. This is particularly true in the case of the risen Jesus since we are dealing with a directly transcendent reality.

Thus, when the apostles describe the impact of this transforming experience in terms of "seeing", "touching", "eating" and "talking" it is important to realise that they are describing in the only way possible from the side of man how the transcendent reality of the risen Jesus could impinge upon their consciousness. These descriptions, however, must not be taken as definitions of the transcendent reality itself. Indeed the appropriateness of attributing in the literal sense physical characteristics such as limbs and senses to the risen Jesus must at least be questioned.[33] To be sure the only way that a transcendent reality could communicate with man is in and through the physical senses of man. This does not necessitate however that the transcendent reality has matching physical senses through which it communicates with man. It is important to remember in this regard that there is a fundamental distinction between a reality and the language which expresses this reality, between an event and the experience which communicates this event, between an objective fact and the subjective assimilation of this fact. The reality, the event, and the fact always contain more than the expression, the experience or the assimilation can indicate.[34]

This point may become clearer if we turn to the transforming experience of Paul by the risen Jesus on the road to Damascus. This experience of Paul is dramatically described in terms of a light, a voice from heaven, and being struck to the ground (*Acts 9:3-9; 22:6-11; 26:13-18*). However, in spite of these colourful descriptions nobody seriously thinks of the risen Jesus in this instance as just a flash of lightning or a voice from heaven. In the same way we should be careful not to reduce the risen Jesus of the gospels to the physical categories of limbs and senses even if these may have been the medium of the transforming experience. This is not to deny the symbolic appropriateness from the side of man of employing such physical categories in order to get across the realness of the experience. This type of symbolic dramatisation often takes place in ordinary life to highlight the uniqueness of a personal experience. In such cases the symbolic quality of our dramatised description is taken for granted.

Another important dimension to the question, What really happened after the death of Jesus?, is that of trying to relate man's contemporary experience of himself to the reality of resurrection. Indeed the real issue for us today is not whether the disciples could physically touch the body of the risen Jesus but rather where, or at what point in man's experience, does the resurrection of Jesus strike a recognisable resonance? To answer this question one must begin with man's present experience and then move back from this as the context in which one assimilates the meaning of the resurrection of Jesus.

Man is a being who looks to the future in terms of human fulfilment and personal completion. In doing so he experiences himself as one who is seeking and searching for permanency, endurance, and personal enlargement. As such these experiences are coloured by the existence of an underlying ambiguity in life itself. On the one hand man experiences moments of joy, fulfilment, and transformation; moments in which, if you like, he steps outside the temporal into the eternal. On the other hand, however, these moments of fullness are all too frequently eclipsed by negative experiences; experiences of death through loss of loved ones, death through the existence of tragedy, death through the reality of guilt and sin. In response there wells up within the being of every individual a desire to overcome death through life, sorrow through joy, absurdity through meaning, and tragedy through indestructibility. In a word, man hopes; he yearns for some form of wholesome fulfilment and personal conquest. As such these different experiences are experiences of the whole man and not simply of the "spirit" or that which we might call "the soul".

It is within the context and from the foreground of these fragmented experiences that the real question about resurrection in terms of what happened after the death of Jesus truly belongs. Have these human aspirations which we find deeply embedded in the heart of man ever been realised? Are the experiences of life, joy, meaning, and indestructibility merely an illusion? Is the hope of man simply a wishful projection without any basis in reality or even worse without any word from God? Is it not reasonable to ask whether there is any point within the history of mankind in which these deeply-rooted aspirations and hopes of mankind have been fulfilled and realised? Is it not precisely an answer to these questions that is at stake when we ask about what happened after the death of Jesus and try to understand the meaning of the resurrection?

It is from the perspective of these questions that assertions about the resurrection of Jesus begin to make sense. Within such an horizon the resurrection appears not as some exception or isolated incident but rather as the realisation and crystallisation of man's deepest aspirations. The resurrection of Jesus from the dead is not just a fake nor is it some kind of trick that was suddenly pulled off at the last moment to salvage a hard-luck story, nor is it a violation of the laws of nature. Rather the resurrection is, in the case of Jesus, the full realisation and actual fulfilment of those seeds of indestructibility which exist within the heart of every individual. It was the blossoming forth of these seeds of indestructibility within the whole man Jesus after death that the apostles were trying to communicate, in proclaiming the resurrection of Jesus from the dead. It would have been impossible for the apostles to make such a bold and extraordinary claim unless they had been compelled to do so by a real experience of the living, personal, and transformed presence of Jesus after his death.

Having made this exploration into the different elements relating to what happened after the death of Jesus, it must be admitted that in the case of the resurrection we are dealing with an experience the totality of which is more than the sum of its individual parts.

5 The mystery of the resurrection: a theological response

We have examined the life, death and resurrection of Jesus from a historical point of view. In doing so we were in fact mapping out the historical foundations of the Christ-Event. It is now time to draw out the theological implications of these historical foundations.

It is important to recall at this stage that it was the words and deeds of the historical Jesus which gave rise to his death and that it was against the background of his death that the mystery of the resurrection unfolded itself for the apostles. No one incident in the life of Jesus can be singled out as definitive in meaning. Neither his words and deeds, nor his death, nor the resurrection taken in isolation from each other make complete christological sense. Instead these different moments in the life of Jesus are bound up intrinsically into a single historical picture which provides the basic material for theological reflection. Within this chapter the determining horizon of our reflection will be the resurrection, not in isolation from the rest of the life of Jesus, but as that reality which comes at the end, encapsulating the overall thrust of the preaching and teaching of the historical Jesus.

The biblical background to resurrection

To fully appreciate the theological import of resurrection in the life of Jesus we must know something about the biblical background to resurrection. For the average Jew, life was a gift from Yahweh whereas sickness and death were caused by some evil power lying in wait for man. Within this precarious balance between life and death it was Yahweh who distributed the gift of life. Length of days was regarded as a blessing from Yahweh and a short life the result of a divine curse. Thus, it is Yahweh who brings back to life the sick man who has fallen under the sway of death.

> Come, let us return to the Lord;
> For he has torn, that he may heal us;
> He has stricken and he will bind us up.
> After two days he will revive us;
> On the third day he will raise us up,
> that we may live before him (*Hos 6:1-2*).

Gradually this power of bringing back to life from sickness is extended. It is no longer just confined to this historical existence but also includes the hereafter in some mysterious way. Traces of this can be found in the exilic dry bones prophecy of *Ezechiel 37:1-14*. Here the spirit of Yahweh is depicted as breathing upon the bones of the dead and bringing them back to life. As such it is only Yahweh who can raise up the dead from the underground place called Sheol.[1]

These primitive ideas concerning the hereafter become more explicitly developed in the post-exilic period—an era in which apocalyptic thought begins to flourish. Here there emerges an expectation of the general resurrection of the dead. This expectation is associated with the end of time and the advent of salvation. As such, this outlook constitutes the essence of Jewish apocalyptic hope. For instance the Apocalypse of *Isaiah,* chapter twenty-six, talks about the end of time when there will be a general judgment (*v. 9*) and then goes on to point out:

> Thy dead shall live, their bodies shall rise.
> O dwellers in the dust, awake and sing for joy!
> For thy dew is a dew of light
> And on the land of shades thou wilt let it fall
> (*Is 26:19*).

A further refinement of this is found in *Dan 12:1-3* which sees the resurrection of the righteous as an awakening to everlasting life whereas for others it will be an awakening to shame. Similar ideas with a slight variation can also be found in the non-canonical Jewish books of *Enoch 51; Baruch 50; IV Ezra 7:29ff.*

In this way there grew up in late Judaism an apocalyptic expectation of a general resurrection of the dead. Although this apocalyptic outlook was somewhat ill-defined at this stage there were certain basic characteristics about it which became clear. For one thing the resurrection of the dead was understood as an act of God, since the God of Israel was a God of the living. Further, the resurrection of the dead to life was something that would occur at the end of time when the final judgment of God would take place. In addition it was a *general* resurrection that was expected in the sense that it would include all members of mankind. The precise nature of this general resurrection at the end of time was a matter of dispute. For some, it was understood in a rather materialistic way with the suggestion that the dead would rise with their bodily infirmities, fully clothed in the way they had died. For others, the resurrection would involve some form of transformation.[2] It was this latter view that seems to have been the more accepted one.

It should be noted here in passing that although it may be argued that the origin of Jewish thinking on resurrection may be traced back to contact with the Persian world, the ultimate source inspiring this apocalyptic hope would have been the experience of the chosen people in their relationship with Yahweh. This experience, fundamentally speaking would include the same type of experiences which we described in our last chapter as part of the context for understanding the resurrection of Jesus, viz. the human experience of hope and the deep-seated aspirations in the heart of man for personal fulfilment. In the context of the chosen people of God these experiences would have included things like national survival and the need for permanency in their relationship with Yahweh. In turn these experiences would be incorporated into their understanding of God as a God of promises and a God who is faithful to his promises.[3]

Within the New Testament period there is considerable evidence for the existence of this apocalyptic hope concerning the general resurrection of the dead at the end of time. We know for instance that the resurrection was a bone of contention between the Pharisees and the Sadducees. The Pharisees accepted the general resurrection of the dead at the end of time whereas the Sadducees rejected it (*Mk 12:18*). When Jesus is consulted about this dispute he asserts not only the reality of the resurrection against the Sadducees but also goes on to point out that those who are raised from the dead "neither marry nor are given in marriage but are like angels in heaven" (*Mk 12:25*). Jesus also seems to be rejecting by implication any materialistic conception of the resurrection that might have been around at that time.[4] Indeed much of the teaching of Jesus incorporates unto itself the perspectives of Jewish apocalyptic thought. This can be seen in his preaching of the Kingdom of God and its future realisation which will involve a definite judgment (*Mt 8:11, 12; 24:30-31; 25:31-32*) and a resurrection of the righteous "who shall shine like the sun in the kingdom of their Father" (*Mt 13:43*). Again in John's gospel there are many references to the resurrection of the just unto eternal life : ". . . the hour is coming when the dead will hear his voice and come forth, those who have done good to the resurrection of life" (*Jn 5:28*). Again "he who eats my flesh and drinks my blood has eternal life, and I will raise him up on the last day" (*Jn 6:54;* cf. also *Jn 6:39, 40, 44*). Although these verses have been worked over theologically by the Johannine school they can still be taken as providing an authentic echo of the historical teaching of Jesus.[5]

There can be no doubt that Jesus would have included himself as a participant in these apocalyptic promises. Not only that, but as time went on he would have understood himself as bound up mysteriously in some way or other with the realisation of these apocalyptic hopes in his capacity as eschatological representative of Yahweh. To this extent Jesus would have seen himself as sharing in the general resurrection of the dead at the end of time in whatever way it would occur according to the designs of Yahweh. However, it is extremely unlikely that he foresaw his own individual resurrection as a distinct and separate event prior to the general resurrection of the dead at the end of time.[6]

By way of conclusion to this examination of the biblical background to the resurrection it is both interesting and instructive to note that it is against the background of Jewish apocalyptic hope that Paul discusses the resurrection of Jesus. He points out that "if there is no resurrection of the dead, then Christ has not been raised" (1 Cor 15:13). This means in effect that if you do not accept the apocalyptic expectation of a general resurrection of the dead then you will have no chance in understanding the individual resurrection of Jesus from the dead. A more shortsighted and less biblical approach to the resurrection would be inclined to say that because Jesus has been raised from the dead you can expect a general resurrection of the dead in the future. Instead Paul puts it the other way around beginning with the given apocalyptic expectation of the resurrection of the dead as the central context for understanding the individual resurrection of Jesus from the dead and then goes on to clarify this future general resurrection of mankind in the light of the resurrection of Jesus. Without this biblical background the resurrection of Jesus from the dead is in danger of being lost.

The overall impact of the resurrection experience

We can now begin to draw out the theological implications of the resurrection experience upon the apostles' understanding of the life of Jesus. In this way we will discover how the Christ-Event came into being as something rooted in the historical experience of the life, death, and resurrection by the apostles and the inherent theological significance of this particular experience. There is a double context in which the resurrection experience takes place, namely the immediate context of the historical life of Jesus and the proximate context of the biblical background on general resurrection.

We have seen how the words and deeds in the life of Jesus marked him out as a unique figure within the history of Judaism. We also saw that these words and deeds were extremely suggestive and that they evoked a deep response from his followers in terms of hopeful Jewish faith. Moreover we saw that there was a certain ambiguity surrounding these words and deeds and that the death of Jesus created a serious challenge for the disciples.

Within this context the inbreaking of the resurrection added a new and unexpected dimension to the significance of the life of Jesus.[7] As such the resurrection of Jesus from the dead can only be understood as the explicit divine seal of approval, recognition, and confirmation of everything Jesus had said and done. The ambiguity that surrounded the life of Jesus and the challenge of the cross is now gradually displaced. The full implications of the words and deeds of the historical Jesus as well as the meaning of his death begin to dawn upon the apostles in the light of the resurrection.

For the first time the apostles find themselves in a confident and reassuring position in which they can establish the personal identity and nature of Jesus that had eluded them up to now. The dynamic and yet mysterious relationship between Jesus and the God whom he dared to address as Abba—Father, begins to unfold itself upon them.

The formulation of this relationship between Jesus and the monotheistic God of Judaism took place in various stages. It was facilitated primarily through the application of different biblical titles to the person of Jesus in the light of the resurrection experience. Jesus is now recognised clearly and unambiguously as the Christ. Furthermore he is identified as the Son of Man, the Suffering Servant, the Son of God, the Lord, the Son of David, and eventually as the Word. These titles initially at least were functional. They described what Jesus had done—he was the suffering servant; what Jesus is doing—he is the reigning Lord; what Jesus will do—he will come as the Son of Man to judge the world. Gradually these titles, through the experience of prayer and worship, took on a confessional dimension. They specified what it meant to be a Christian, viz. one who confessed Jesus to be the Christ and Lord. Eventually with the expansion of Christianity into the Hellenistic world the ontological implications of both function and confession were spelled out. In this way through a process of historical growth and theological development under the inspiration of the Holy Spirit, the personal identity and nature of Jesus in terms of divinity introduces itself into the apostolic Church. This came about through an emphasis on the exalted and heavenly condition of Jesus which pointed towards his divine origin and destiny.

Once the divinity of Jesus is accepted, no matter how gradually, the idea of Jesus as both God and man begins to dawn upon the apostles. This in turn paves the way for laying the foundations for the doctrine of the Incarnation which sees Jesus as the Word made flesh (*Jn 1:4*). Finally the doctrine of the Incarnation points towards the pre-existence of Jesus (*Jn 1:1; Phil 2:5ff*) and raises the whole question of his relationship to creation within the plan of salvation (*Col 1:15-20; Rom 8:19-22; Eph 1:9-10; 22:23*).

The catalyst triggering off this rich development of ideas, many of which were implicitly present in the words and deeds of Jesus, was the mystery of the resurrection. It will be noticed here that the basic tenets of traditional christology such as the messiahship, the divinity, the Incarnation, and the pre-existence of Jesus come at the end as conclusions to our historical examination of the life, death and resurrection of Jesus. This does not mean that these "high" qualities are simply adopted at a subsequent stage in our reflections on the life of Jesus. Rather they are qualities that were there from the beginning which only come into full view through the gradual revelation that was taking place historically and progressively throughout the life, death, and resurrection of Jesus. To this extent it should be clear that the resurrection coupled with the outpouring of the Holy Spirit at Pentecost constitutes the final stage in our transition from a low-ascending christology to a fully developed "high" christology.

In addition to the words and deeds of Jesus which provide the immediate context for understanding the impact of the resurrection experience upon the apostles there is also the proximate context of Jewish apocalyptic hope as centred around the resurrection of the dead at the end of time. Within this context the resurrection of Jesus from the dead stands out as that unique event which fulfils this Jewish apocalyptic hope by anticipating its future realisation. Because Jesus has been raised from the dead it is now clear that he is the personal realisation of the end of time understood in terms of judgment and resurrection which have now taken place in him.[8] That a single individual should anticipate the realisation of the end of time in this particular way surpassed the expectations of Jewish apocalyptic thought. That the final resurrection of "the last day" should occur in and through the resurrection of an individual "was a preposterously novel idea—clearly unthinkable for any Jew who had not been compelled to it by experience".[9] For one thing it had been

a general resurrection of all men that they had expected
and not that of a single individual. Furthermore, most
Jewish apocalyptic thought was characterised by a cosmic
upheaval that would inaugurate the end. Instead, this
cosmic drama is now understood to have taken place in
the personal and corporeal resurrection of Jesus from the
dead—an event that is not without its own cosmic significance as symbolised in the idea of Jesus as the "New
Creation" (2 Cor 5:17). In this way it becomes clear to the
apostles through their experience of the resurrection that
Jesus is the individual fulfilment, personal realisation and
historical anticipation of Jewish apocalyptic hope—an insight which was the inspiring source of many new horizons
in the early Church.

Because Jesus is the individual fulfilment of the end
of time it can be said that he is the climax of God's self-
revelation to mankind in history.[10] God can only fully
reveal himself at the end of the process through which he
has chosen to reveal himself. This process through which
God has chosen to reveal himself is historical, particularly
the history of the chosen people and most of all the history
of the man Jesus. This linear development of history as
the vehicle of God's self-revelation was something peculiar
to the religious traditions of Judaism.[11] The end of this
revelatory history has been anticipated in the resurrection
of Jesus from the dead. Therefore to that extent the self-
revelation of God in history has been anticipated and
realised in Jesus. In other words the history of God's
dealings with the chosen people of Israel reached a high-
point in the resurrection of Jesus from the dead. This
high-point is now seen as the completion of God's promises as enshrined in the traditions of Israel. Not only that,
but this high-point is experienced as the dawning of the
end of the world and is therefore understood as the
supreme and decisive moment of God's self-revelation
within history.

Also arising out of this understanding of Jesus as the

personal realisation of the end of time is the presence of
a new outlook on eschatology. Because Jesus has been
raised from the dead he is the eschatological fullness of
salvation; that is to say he embodies the advent of God's
promise of salvation to mankind. As the fullness of salvation
he is "the beginning of the end" in that the end time of
salvation (the *Eschaton*) has now appeared historically in
and through the resurrection of Jesus from the dead. This
historical appearance of salvation in Jesus inaugurates a
new era of salvation which will only be fully completed in
the second coming of Christ. Thus, Jesus as the risen Christ
is "the first fruits" (*1 Cor 15:20*) of God's eschatological
harvest which is now in the reaping. As the "first fruits"
the resurrection of Jesus from the dead is a preview event
signalling liberation and summoning man to future salvation through resurrection.[12] Lastly because the end time has
been historically anticipated in Jesus this means that the
Kingdom of God has come upon earth in and through the
resurrection of Jesus from the dead. The tension between
the past and present, between promise and fulfilment in the
preaching of Jesus, especially in relation to the Kingdom
of God, has now been resolved through the personal resurrection of Jesus from the dead. In particular the eschatological suggestiveness of the claims made by Jesus in proclaiming the Kingdom of God has now not only been
realised but also verified. As a result the Kingdom and
nearness of God on earth has been set up in Jesus as the
risen Christ. This reign of God in the risen Jesus is communicated historically through the community we call the
Church. This community, composed of followers of Jesus
Christ, celebrates in the world through Word and Sacrament, in hopeful faith, the Kingdom of God on earth as
present reality in Jesus and as future promise to those who
belong to Jesus.

Different christological responses to the Easter Event

Over and above this general description of the impact of the resurrection experience upon the apostles it is also possible to break down the New Testament picture of Jesus into different christological steps and stages. These progressive christological phases reflect the influence of different cultural strands operating upon the formation and development of the Christ-Event in the New Testament period. These cultural strands as already noted in chapter two may be broadly classified as Palestinian, Jewish-Hellenistic and Hellenistic-Gentile. In each of these different cultural situations Christian communities came into being and in doing so they formulated their own understanding of the significance of the life, death and resurrection of Jesus. In each case it is the Easter experience that provides the foundation-stone in their formulation of the Christ-Event.

In the Palestinian community it is the nearness and realness of the resurrection experience that determines their understanding of Jesus. Because of this closeness to the resurrection experience their hopes are propelled towards the imminence of the second coming of Jesus in the Parousia. As a result most of the thinking at this early stage is futuristic in orientation and this is reflected in the articulation of the Palestinian responses to the Easter Event. The emphasis in these responses is directed towards the early return of Jesus in the light of his resurrection.

Within this framework Jesus is identified as the Son of Man (*Acts 7:55-56*) who is expected to come in power and glory soon. This identification goes back to the original third person Son of Man sayings spoken by Jesus himself (*Mk 8:38; Lk 12:8ff*). This return of Jesus as the Son of Man will be the final and full vindication of everything that the earthly Jesus had said and done.[13] Closely linked with this resurrection-Parousia vision of Jesus is the use of the Aramaic formula "Our Lord, Come"/*Maranatha*

(*1 Cor 16:22; Apoc 22:20*). This very early formula was used as an invocatory prayer addressed to Jesus, most probably in a eucharistic context, as a plea for his immediate return in the Parousia.[14]

By far the most important and certainly the most central category of Palestinian christology was that of the Christ-messiah category. Here, as with the Son of Man and "Our Lord, Come" designations, the recognition of Jesus as the Christ takes place first of all in a futuristic framework of resurrection-Parousia.[15] This earliest Palestinian christology talked about Jesus returning at the Parousia as "the Christ appointed for you" (*Acts 3:20*). It was this recognition of Jesus as the Christ more than any other that summed up symbolically everything that could be said to a first century Jew about Jesus of Nazareth and yet the acceptance of Jesus as the messiah who would appear at the Parousia required a certain amount of rethinking by Jewish converts in the light of the historical life of Jesus, especially the scandal of the cross.

Because Jesus will be the messiah he is also seen futuristically by the Palestinian community as the "Son of David" (*Apoc 3:7; 5:5*) and the "Son of God" (*Lk 1:32*) who will appear at the Parousia.[16] Within Judaism it was expected that a descendant of David would inaugurate the messianic era (*Mk 11:10*)—a fact which explains the christological importance of the genealogies in Matthew and Luke who trace the descent of Jesus back through David (*Mt 1:1-17; Lk 3:23-38*). As for the title "Son of God" this was a biblical way of expressing the closeness of relationship between an individual and Yahweh not unlike the English designation of a person as "a man of God". In the Old Testament we find individuals and groups being called son(s) of God (*Ex 4:22ff; Hos 11:1; Is 1:2, 30:1, 63:16; Jer 3:19ff*). Around the time of pre-Christian Judaism "Son of God" came into use as a messianic title. Its application to Jesus at this early stage was functional, being based on the logical implications of the messianic status of Jesus[17] (*Mk 8:29; Mt 16:16*). It was only at a much later Hellenistic stage that this title assumed metaphysical connotations.

The other significant title within Palestinian christology at this stage was the designation of Jesus as the "Mosaic prophet-servant of Yahweh".[18] This would seem to be a fusion of the "eschatological prophet" category with other ideas prominent in the life of Jesus such as the Isaiah servant theme and the Jesus-Moses parallel. This synthetic designation of Jesus as the "Mosaic prophet-servant" of Yahweh was used to explain the earthly historical life of Jesus. Echoes of this can be found in the early sermon of Peter in *Acts 3:12-26* which talks about God raising up a prophet (*vv. 22-24*) and a servant (*v. 26*) after the manner of Moses (*v. 22*) to turn the people from their wickedness (*v. 26*). In spite of these subsequent developments, however, the central christological category at this stage is the recognition of Jesus as the Christ around which these other titles are built up. It was this outstanding designation that summed up the Christ-Event for Palestinian Jewish Christianity.

Alongside this early Palestinian community there emerged also the existence of a Jewish-Hellenistic Church which was composed of Greek-speaking Jewish Christian converts. This development involved the complex question of translating Palestinian categories into understandable Hellenistic categories. This was facilitated primarily through the use of the Greek Septuagint version of the Old Testament. Within this transition there took place an important and significant theological shift in which emphasis on the future Parousia was redirected back to the present importance of the exaltation of Jesus. This shift was inspired by the delay of the Parousia. In the Palestinian community Jesus is the one who will appear as the Christ in the Parousia whereas now it emerges in the Hellenistic-Jewish Church that Jesus has already been appointed Lord and Christ (*Acts 2:36*) in virtue of his

exaltation at the resurrection. The emphasis now is on the
present status of Jesus as the one reigning over the community of his followers in the light of his exaltation
through resurrection.

The central category through which this change is
emphasised is that of "Lord"/*Kyrios*. Jesus is now known
and proclaimed as the reigning Lord. By calling Jesus
"Lord" the Greek-speaking Jews were transferring a
title to Jesus which in the Greek Old Testament had been
used to translate the Hebrew equivalent for Yahweh. The
implications of this transfer will be examined in our next
chapter. For the moment it is sufficient to note that from
now on the basic proclamation of the Greek-speaking
Jewish community is that "Jesus is Lord" (*Acts 11:20,
16:31; Phil 2:11*) and it is in the name of the "Lord
Jesus" that people are baptised (*Acts 8:16, 19:5*). Quite
often this basic proclamation is linked up with the central
category of the Palestinian Church of Jesus as the Christ
so that taken together these two designations provide us
with a succinct summary of the Christian creed in terms
of "Jesus Christ our Lord" *(Acts 2:36; 11:17)*.[19] In a
somewhat similar vein the other Palestinian titles of "Son
of Man", "Son of David" and "Son of God" are applied
to Jesus first and foremost as the exalted and reigning
Lord (*Rom 1:3-4*). At a later stage there are the beginnings
of a tendency within the Jewish-Hellenistic Church to
project these titles back into the earthly life of Jesus.

The third and final development of New Testament
christology arises within the directly Hellenistic Christian
community. This takes place under the inspiration of the
missionary activity of the Pauline and Johannine schools
of theology Within this new situation the Church accom-
modates herself to the thought patterns of the Hellenistic
world. The classical description of this development can
be found in *Phil 2:6-11*. This important christological
hymn is set out within the three-storied Hellenistic world-
view of heaven, earth, and the underworld (*v. 10*). This

setting provides what is popularly known as a three-stage christology of pre-existence (*v. 6*), Incarnation (*vv. 7-8*), and exaltation (*vv. 9-11*).[20] This three-fold pattern is developed with slight variations by the Greek-speaking world in different christological hymns. For instance in *Col 1:15-20* the pre-existence of Jesus Christ is expanded upon by drawing out his relationship with creation in terms of being "the first born of all creation" (*v. 15*) and therefore the actual agent through whom "all things were created" (*v. 16*). Another variation of this basic pattern is found in the prologue of John's gospel (*Jn 1:1-14*). This begins with the pre-existence of the Word (*v. 1-4*) and leads up to a climax with the Incarnation of the Word in Jesus as a manifestation of divine glory (*v. 14*).

A further characteristic of Hellenistic christology is the presence of a definite tendency to push the exaltation of Jesus back into his earthly ministry so that the glory of the post-paschal period is thought to have been present in a veiled form throughout the historical life. Instances of this can be found in the Infancy narratives, the baptismal accounts, and the transfiguration scenes of the synoptics. This projection back is particularly evident in John's gospel which has a very developed "high" christology.

Finally, there is a development in the usage of the various biblical titles. The "Son of Man" designations of the earlier christologies now take on a pre-existent dimension assuming a descending and ascending role (*Jn 3:13; 6:62*). The term "Christ" loses its titular force and becomes largely a proper name for Jesus. The title "Lord"/*Kyrios* grows in importance, taking on more than a purely functional significance. Lastly, "Son of God" becomes a popular designation and acquires meaning which exceeds its biblical background.

This bare outline of the different christological responses to the Easter experience gives us some idea of the development taking place in the New Testament formulation of the Christ-Event. At times the lines of development are blurred and therefore one should not be too clinical in trying to dissect the different stages of development in New Testament christology.

6 Discovering the implications of the Christ-Event

It should now be quite clear that Jesus was only fully recognised as the Christ who is the Lord in and through the mystery of the resurrection. The Christ-Event therefore is something that came into being as a result of the resurrection and Pentecostal experiences. The working out of the universal significance of the Christ-Event, which we have already described as the other side of the mystery of Jesus Christ, took time to unfold itself within the experience and understanding of the early Church. In fact it took several hundred years before the Church could formally define this universal significance. It is this universal significance of the Christ-Event for our understanding of God, man and the universe, that we must now take up. The foundations for this universal significance have been laid down in the New Testament through the different christological formulations of the Christ-Event which we examined in our last chapter. The central issue in working out the universal significance of the Christ-Event is that of the relationship which exists between Jesus and God or that which is more commonly referred to as the divinity of Jesus. It is this basic issue that we must now examine with special reference to the New Testament evidence.

In what way did Jesus see himself related to God? How did the early Church describe this relationship between Jesus and God? To what extent do these descriptions of the relationship between Jesus and God allow us to talk about the divinity of Jesus or even to refer to Jesus as God? That Jesus is referred to as God in the New Testament is beyond doubt. What is not sufficiently

considered quite often is the cautious manner in which
the explicit confession of Jesus as God is made in the
New Testament. To fully appreciate this cautious development within the New Testament period we will try to trace
the early Church's experience and understanding of the
divinity of Jesus up to the explicit designation of Jesus
as God.

Jesus as Lord

There can be no discussion of this issue or indeed of any
issue in christology that does not contain some reference
to the earthly life of the historical Jesus. In the context of
the question under review we ʰave seen that the different
words and deeds of the historical Jesus marked him out as a
"man of God" (a biblical son of God) who had a very close
and real relationship with God. This emerges in a variety
of different ways throughout the life of the historical Jesus
which we can only briefly touch upon here at this stage.
We have already seen something of the relationship between
Jesus and God in the preaching of Jesus which announces
the Kingdom of God. This proclamation of the Kingdom
by Jesus had eschatological implications about the end of
time and the advent of salvation. The person chosen by
God to bring about these implications is Jesus and this
clearly implies a real closeness between Jesus and God.
Further we also saw something of the nearness between
Jesus and God in the claims that Jesus made to authority.
In particular by claiming to forgive sins and to fulfil the
Mosaic Law Jesus seemed to be assuming certain divine
prerogatives. Last and most significant is the description
by Jesus of this relationship between himself and God in
terms of a father-son relationship in which Jesus addresses
God as Father. The whole life style of the pre-Easter Jesus
suggests a special filial bond between Jesus as Son and
God as Father. This is brought out clearly by the theocentric attitude of Jesus throughout his earthly life.[1]

It is against this background that the early Church's consciousness of the divinity of Jesus grew, especially through its articulation of the Christ-Event. There can be no doubt that it was only in the light of the resurrection that a proper understanding of the divinity of Jesus emerged.[2] This development came about through a process of reflection upon the marvellous things that the God of Israel had performed in and through the life, death and resurrection of Jesus. This process of reflection therefore was based on past and present experience of Jesus and it articulated itself through the ascription of different titles to Jesus in formulating the Christ-Event. The particular titles which are of most interest in regard to the relationship between Jesus and God are the titles "Lord" (*Kyrios*) and "God" (*Theos*).

Because the earliest formulation of the Christ-Event in the Palestinian community was centred around Jesus as the Christ who is to come in the Parousia it would seem that the particular question of the precise relationship between Jesus and God did not arise explicitly at this early stage.[3] It would have been present in latent form only by way of implication without however receiving any formal expression. It was only with the shift in theological perspective from the future Parousia to the present exaltation that the precise issue about the status of Jesus came into focus. If Jesus is now experienced and understood as the reigning Exalted One then the question of his relationship with God introduces itself. This question as we know is resolved by confessing Jesus as Lord/*Kyrios*. This particular confession was a major christological advance, the implications of which took time to be fully absorbed. To understand these implications a brief summary of the background leading to this breakthrough is necessary. The use of the title "Lord" in reference to Jesus occurs at different times with different nuances of meaning throughout the first century.[4] It began in the life of the historical Jesus. Here we discover that Jesus is referred to as "Lord"

(Aramaic *Mari*).[5] At this stage the word "Lord" is used as a polite and courteous mode of address not unlike "Master" or "Rabbi".[6] This use of the word "Lord" indicated the recognition of human authority and the existence of a close bond between those who used it and the person addressed.[7] In the case of Jesus this usage would have stemmed from the suggestiveness of his words and deeds, especially in their authoritative bearing.

In the post-Paschal Palestinian Church this title is developed into the prayer formula of "Our Lord, Come" (*Maranatha*) addressed to Jesus. This development acknowledges not only the authority of Jesus in his earthly ministry but also recognises the exalted rank of the one who is to come in the Parousia. In particular this development is informed by the central messianic category of Jesus as the Christ. To this extent the primitive christological designation of Jesus as Lord by the Palestinian community cannot be understood as conferring divine status or expressing divinity in any real sense at this stage. Instead the title "Lord" in this context is concerned with the authoritative function and status of Jesus as the one who is to come.[8]

It was out of this primitive Palestinian tradition that the Hellenistic-Jewish presentation of Jesus as Lord grew and assumed real divine significance. This major christological advance was based on a number of factors. It was derived from the idea of exaltation which now became prominent due to the delay of the Parousia. This idea of exaltation was informed by the application to Jesus of *Psalm 110:1* as shown in *Acts 32:34-37*: "The Lord (Yahweh) said to my Lord (the one of authority), Sit at my right hand, till I make thy enemies a stool for thy feet" (*Acts 2:34-35*).[9] This theme of "sitting at the right hand of God" which is popular in the Pauline letters (*Rom 8:34; Eph 1:20; Col 3:1*) signified a new understanding of the status and dignity of Jesus. Further the proclamation of Jesus as Lord by the Hellenistic-Jewish community served as a translation of the Palestinian tradition which spoke of the earthly Jesus as the one who is to come as "Lord" (*Maranatha*) in the authoritative and messianic sense. In addition this presentation of Jesus as Lord/*Kyrios* employed a title which in the Greek-speaking world of Judaism had been used to circumlocute the divine name of Yahweh.[10] It was the fusion of these different elements that provided the promotion of Jesus as Lord in the Hellenistic-Jewish community.[11] The development of this proclamation which may be represented schematically as follows took place in continuity with the Palestinian tradition while at the same time expanding and enriching its content:

1. The earthly Jesus as Lord—the exalted Jesus as Lord who is to come (*Maranatha*).

2. Jesus as Lord/*Kyrios*

(a) Exaltation: Psalm *110:1;*

(b) Translation of (1);

(c) Influence of the LXX.

The Greek word for Lord—*Kyrios*—was a title of honour signifying the authority of a superior over an inferior within the social and political domain. By using this Greek title to circumlocute the name of Yahweh in reading aloud the Greek version of the Old Testament the Hellenistic speaking Jews attached to the secular word "Lord"/*Kyrios* "a whole complex of associations going far beyond its sociological meaning in Greek and implying a whole Yahwistic theology of covenant and redemptive history".[12] It is this new range of associations which are now transferred to Jesus by the Hellenistic-Jewish community. The transfer at this stage is primarily functional[13] and it implies that the functions of Yahweh will now be exercised in and through the reigning exalted Jesus.

Following close upon this major christological

insight was the further expansion of Jesus as Lord within the Gentile world. The clearest example here is the christological hymn of *Phil 2:5-11*, where we are told that the exalted Jesus is given "the name which is above every name" (*v. 9*), that this name is Lord/*Kyrios*, and that as the exalted one he should be worshipped by all (*v. 10*). The significant factor here is the transference to Jesus as the exalted one of the divine name of God which is above every name.[14] Clearly God is now present exercising his lordship over the universe in and through Jesus Christ as the exalted Lord. Quite obviously this development of Jesus as Lord goes beyond the purely functional role of Jesus in the Hellenistic-Jewish communities.

Jesus and God

If Jesus could now be consciously and deliberately given the rich title "Lord/*Kyrios*" with all its implications, why not go the whole way and call him "God" (*Theos*)? The answer to this question is that the early Church did eventually refer to Jesus as God but that this specific designation came at a later stage in the latter half of the first century. Before taking up this point, however, it is important to note the delicate development that was actually taking place through the proclamation of Jesus as Lord and through the emerging theology of Paul, both of which pave the way for the ultimate designation of Jesus as God.

In this regard it must be remembered that Christianity was growing up under the controlling influence of Judaism. One of the outstanding characteristics of Judaism was its strong monotheism which restricted the use of the word "God". Within this atmosphere the word "God" with its strict monotheistic connotations was too narrow to be applied to Jesus.[15] Instead the word "God" in the New Testament period referred primarily to God the Father[16] whom Jesus addressed in prayer and who raised Jesus from the dead. To call Jesus "God" within this situation therefore would have been too sudden a transition. Furthermore any such designation could easily have appeared to border on blasphemy for early Christian Jews. Moreover this strong monotheistic climate was perpetuated by the fact that the first Christian Jews continued to frequent the Jewish temple in Jerusalem. This fact alone would have made it an *anathema* to call Jesus "God". As a result this close contact with Jewish monotheism would have had a controlling influence upon the infant Church as it tried to work out its specifically Christian doctrine of God.

At the other end of the spectrum there existed within the Hellenistic world a strong presence of polytheism. To call Jesus "God" here would be to run the risk of complete misunderstanding. It could easily give the impression of presenting Jesus as just another god alongside all the other different Hellenistic gods. In the theology of Paul we find a sharp sensitivity to the possibility of being misunderstood by these two extremes. This sensitivity explains the presence of bipartite confessional formulae in the writings of Paul in which he affirms the oneness of God alongside the unique mediating Lordship of Jesus. A good example of this can be found in *1 Cor 8:5-6* : "For although there may be so-called gods in heaven or on earth—as indeed there are many 'gods' and many 'lords'—yet for us there is one God, the Father, . . . and one Lord, Jesus Christ, through whom are all things and through whom we exist." (Cf. also *Ep 4:5; 1 Tim 2:5; Gal 3:20*).

Within this situation the confession of Jesus as Lord acts as a bridge to the later designation of Jesus as God.[17] Initially this confession of Jesus as Lord in the Hellenistic-Jewish Church was sufficiently nuanced as to eliminate any offence to the monotheism of the Jews and avoid the polytheism of the pagan world. As we have already seen, the Greek word for Lord—*Kyrios*—had a wide range of meaning varying from that of human authoritative significance up to personal divinity as used in reading the Septuagint. Once the full implications of Lord/*Kyrios* became clear as they did in the Hellenistic community the time would have been opportune for the full designation of God/*Theos*.[18]

Also acting as a bridge here would have been the developments taking place in the writings of Paul. We have already noted Paul's careful construction of bipartite confessional formulae. In addition Paul institutes parallelisms between Jesus Christ and God which allows him to speak interchangeably about the "Spirit of God" and the "Spirit of Christ"; the "love of Christ" and the "love of God" (*Rom 8:9, 35, 39*). Further, Paul presents a picture of Jesus Christ as the one who is God's agent in creation (*1 Cor 8:6; Col 1:16*), who is the "form" (*Phil 2:6*) and "image" (*2 Cor 4:4; Col 1:5*) of God, who reflects the "glory" of God (*2 Cor 4:6*), and in whom the fullness of God was pleased to dwell (*Col 1:19*). These rich developments in Paul's theology also paved the way for calling Jesus God later on in the first century.

In the light of this delicate development that was taking place through the early Church's proclamation of Jesus as Lord and the theology of Paul we can now move on to examine those instances in which Jesus is acknowledged as God. The declaration of Jesus as God only occurs explicitly and unequivocally in three clear cases in the New Testament.[19] Two of these are to be found in the fourth gospel. The prologue of John's gospel commences with the Word that existed in the beginning alongside God and who was God (*v. 1*). From here the prologue goes on to identify "the Word made flesh" with Jesus (*v. 14*). In addition there is also the well-known confession of doubting Thomas which acknowledges Jesus as "My Lord and my God" (*Jn 20:28*) which is probably the clearest reference to Jesus as God. Thirdly, the author of Hebrews quotes *Psalm 45:6-7* in such a way that God becomes a title for Jesus. The expressions "Thy throne, O God, is forever" and ". . . therefore thy God, O God, has anointed thee" (*v. 9*) are taken to refer to Jesus. In each case the vocative "O God" is addressed directly to Jesus.

In addition there are five other instances in which Jesus is probably called God. These are : *Jn 1:18; Tit 2:13; 1 Jn 5:20; Rom 9:5; 2 Pt 1:1.* These probable instances are not always clear and require a careful exegetical exposition which cannot be gone into here.[20] Lastly, there are other texts—*Gal 2:20; Acts 20:28; 2 Thess 1:12*—which do allude to Jesus as God but which at the same time contain so many textual variations and linguistic obscurities in the original manuscripts that they are of no real probative value.

A glance at this evidence shows that Jesus is never called God in the Synoptics or in the early preaching of the *Acts of the Apostles.* Instead most of the evidence, especially the three clear cases in *John* and *Hebrews,* is concentrated in the latter half of the first century. *Hebrews* is a difficult letter to date. Some would situate it in the late sixties, whereas others would locate it in the seventies. The gospel of John is generally accepted as belonging to the nineties.

A significant date here in trying to determine when the early Church came around to calling Jesus "God" is the year 70 A.D. in which the destruction of the temple in Jerusalem took place. It is surely no mere coincidence that references to Jesus as God are most clear after this event. After all, the destruction of the temple necessitated a clear break for Christianity away from the confines of Judaism with its strict Monotheism. This break from the temple would have brought a greater focusing on the need for creating a more specifically Christian form of liturgical prayer and worship. This development would have provided a most suitable setting for referring to Jesus as God. This particular suggestion is borne out both by the textual evidence and by liturgical considerations.

On the textual level four of the probable references to Jesus as God are doxologies addressed to Jesus (*1 Tit*

2:13; 1 Jn 5:20; Rom 9:5; 2 Pt 1:1). Moreover *Hebrews 1:8-10* as already noted applies a psalm to Jesus and we know that the singing of psalms was a common practice in Christian liturgical celebrations (*1 Cor 14:26; Ep 5:19*). In addition John's prologue was originally a hymn and again we know from Pliny the Younger that Christians used to sing hymns as to a God (cf. also *Eph 5:19*). Finally it can be argued that Thomas's declaration probably represents a confessional formula with a liturgical background to it.[21]

On the liturgical level there can be no doubt that this new situation of the infant Church away from the influence of the temple created a new awareness and consciousness in prayer and worship. This awareness would have grown out of their experience of Jesus as Lord who was the underlying power and presence binding them together into a distinct Christian community. Within such a Christian experience the *lex orandi* would have influenced the direction of the *lex credendi*. The doctrinal development of Jesus as God was not just something that arose out of pure intellectual or theological speculation. Rather it emerged as the most adequate articulation of their "felt" liturgical experience. This type of doctrinal development not only clarified their liturgical experience but also enriched it. To this extent it is equally true to say that the *lex credendi* also shaped the *lex orandi*. It was this mutual influence between liturgy and doctrine that would have given rise amongst other factors to the acclamation of Jesus as God.[22]

Alongside this development there would also have been taking place a gradual broadening of the concept of God within the Christian community. Slowly it would have emerged that God revealed so much of himself in the life, death and resurrection of Jesus that the concept of God would have to be able to include both Father and Son. This insight would have been based on the past experience of the preaching and teaching of the historical

Jesus as well as the present experience of the Lordship of Christ in their lives.

We have already seen that in the life of the historical Jesus there developed a close filial relationship between Jesus as Son and God as Father. We find Jesus frequently referring to God as "My Father" (*Lk 22:29; Lk 24:49*) and "Your Father" (*Mt 7:11; Mk 11:25*), in such a way that it becomes quite clear that there is a special relationship between Jesus as Son and God as Father. The description of this relationship in the language of Father-Son is parabolic in origin, being derived from human relationships.[23] It is based on the intimate knowledge that only a father and a son can have of each other. It is precisely this parable of the intimacy that exists between a father and a son which Jesus develops elsewhere[24] that he now invokes to describe his own relationship to God as Father. Gradually this parabolic language is interpreted in a real and proper sense to designate the absolute relationship that exists between Jesus as Son and God as Father. This in turn leads to the absolute language of "the Father" and "the Son". This is most evident as one would expect in the gospel of John, though traces of it may also be found in the Synoptics (*Mk 13:32; Mt 11:27ff*). For John the Word was God (*v. 1*) and the Word became enfleshed in Jesus Christ who is "the only Son of the Father" (*Jn 1:14, 18; 3:16, 18; cf. 1 Jn 4:9*). Throughout the gospel of John Jesus alone is called "the Son" and there exists an intrinsic relation of origin and dependency between "the Father" and "the Son". The Son is sent by the Father, he obeys the Father's commandments (*Jn 5:10*), he can do nothing of his own accord (*Jn 15:19-20*), his words are the Father's (*Jn 14: 10-24; 17:8*) as are his deeds. The end result of this Father-Son relationship is that there is a unity (*Jn 10:30*) between Jesus and God that would seem to be more than a merely moral unity.[25] The terms "the Father" and "the Son" now stand in relationship not only absolutely but also as proper names for God and Jesus. It is this absolute relationship that broadens the concept of God so that an awareness of Jesus not simply as God but as the Son of God distinct from a purely biblical son of God could develop in the early Church.

A final if not somewhat secondary factor promoting this development about the divine status of Jesus would have been the growing custom of an imperial cult within the political sphere. This consisted in emperors, specifically Domitian and to a lesser extent Nero, claiming deification and thereby requiring a corresponding divine worship. It it quite conceivable that this emperor worship, which was being imposed upon Christians and thereby leading to the persecution of those who refused to conform, would have induced the Christian community to assert the true divinity of Jesus (*1 Pt 3:15; Apoc 17:14*) as a corrective to this political abuse.[26]

In this way the early Church articulated its experience and understanding of God in Jesus of Nazareth. It was an articulation that steered an even course between monotheism and polytheism, coming up with its own uniquely inspired doctrine of God in Jesus Christ our Lord.[27] Our examination of the Christ-Event has taken us through a long process of development that began with the historical Jesus as a man and led to the theological confession of Jesus as God. The initial foundations in the New Testament of the universal significance of the Christ-Event that we have been exposing in this chapter were to become the object of theological reflection and heated debate in subsequent centuries. Within this cross-fire of ideas it was to take another four hundred years to iron out clearly the full universal significance of the Christ-Event. It is that period of doctrinal development that we must now take up.

7 Defining the universal significance of the Christ-Event

To confess Jesus Christ as Lord is one thing; to define doctrinally the universal significance of this confession is quite another thing. The real achievement of the Church in the New Testament period was the successful juxtaposing of its Christian faith in "Jesus Christ our Lord" alongside its basic faith in the monotheistic God of Judaism. The big task now facing the Church was the development of this bipartite confession into a more unified picture while at the same time translating the universal significance of "Jesus Christ our Lord" into terms that would be understood by the rest of the world. The purpose of this chapter is to sketch in bare outline some of the different debates during the Patristic period that promoted the realisation of this huge task. These debates, especially in the early centuries, were both trinitarian and christological. Our sketch, however, must confine itself to the specifically christological dimensions of these debates.

It was through the early Church's contact with the Hellenistic world that the deeper philosophical and theological questions about the universal significance of the Christ-Event began to be raised. These questions were already present in the Hellenistic christology of New Testament times. The terms of reference had been laid down through the experience of the apostolic Church and its articulation of that experience in ideas like the universal Lordship of Jesus, the Word made flesh, God as Father, and Jesus as "the Son". With the missionary expansion of the Church into the Gentile world these

94

questions became more acute. In what sense was Jesus the
Son of God? How could the eternal God be present historically in Jesus of Nazareth? What did this mean in a
world that already had its own philosophical understanding of God? How could Christianity mediate and translate
its new understanding of God into this different cultural
situation? How could the Church overcome the "scandal
of particularity" as it moved into this open-ended univer-
salist situation?

The Patristic debate up to Nicea

These questions gradually imposed themselves upon the
consciousness of the Church as it eased its way into a new
socio-cultural situation. The second century has been
rightly described as that period in which the great trans-
position of Christian doctrine took place.[1] This trans-
position involved a transformation[2] of the inherited Jewish
categories of Christianity into the more universal categories of the Hellenistic world. This process of transformation was inspired not only by the intellect but also and
even more fundamentally by the ongoing liturgical experiences of prayer and worship under the guidance of
the Holy Spirit within the Christian community.

The key concept within this process of transformation
was that of the *Logos* which was common to both Judaism
and Greek philosophy. It is extremely difficult to translate
comprehensively into English the rich range of meaning
attached to this word *Logos*. The nearest English render-
ings are "Word" or "Reason". In a certain sense these two
words are only aspects of the same fundamental idea.
The "Word" is that which gives expression to reason and
"Reason" is that which gives meaning to the Word.[3]

Within Judaism the Word was that reality through
which God was active in history. One finds the creative
Word of God active at the beginning of the world (*Gen
1:1ff*). Later on it is this Word of God which communi-

cates itself through the prophets and which calls people back to God within history. At an even later stage this Word of God seems to personify itself in the *Wisdom* literature. For the Jew the Word of God was operative in history unfolding progressively a divine pattern of power, presence, and purpose.

Within the Hellenistic world the "Word" or better "Reason" has a long philosophical lineage to it. It goes back to Heraclitus (d. ca. 500 B.C.), who first uses it as a basic concept within his philosophical system. From there it goes through a series of developments in Platonism, Middle Platonism, and Stoicism. In its mature form the concept of "Reason" referred to an all-pervading principle of rationality underlying the universe. It was the presence of this underlying rationality within the cosmos that made the world go round. It accounted for the origin, the order and meaningfulness of the world we live in. For many it became the basis of religious faith. Thus for the Jew the Word/*Logos* was a form of God's presence active in history whereas for the Greek, Reason/*Logos* was that underlying reality which explained the structure of the universe we live in.[4]

These two different ways of looking at the world we live in were united and transformed by Christianity. The foundations for this development were laid in the first century through the theology of John's gospel which identified Jesus Christ as the Word of God made flesh (*Jn 1:14*). It seems most probable that the Johannine school of scribes would have been familiar with both the Jewish and Hellenistic background to this concept of the Word[5] and would therefore have intended the transformation of these two traditions by identifying Jesus as the personal revelation of the Word. Certainly in the second century the Johannine use of the Word/*Logos* is taken by the Christian apologists to include the Greek concept of Reason/*Logos*. Jesus is now presented as one who embodies the Jewish Word of God and the Hellenistic Reason of ration-

ality in the world. As a result Jesus appears as the key
to both history and the universe. It was this insight that
opened up the way for universalising the significance of
the Christ-Event in the second century. As a result, most
of the christological discussions in this century are centred
around the relationship between the Word and Jesus.

Another basic insight determining the shape of christological discussion in the Patristic period was the acceptance
of the man Jesus as divine even though the implications
of this had yet to be worked out from a philosophical and
theological point of view. This acceptance of the man
Jesus as divine was not intended to subtract in any way
from the full humanity of Jesus. Reactions, however, to
this occurred at two levels. There were those who held that
Jesus only appeared to have a real body and that therefore
he did not really suffer or die. These were known as the
Docetists.

Closely related to the Docetists were the Gnostics who
held that salvation was based on the communication of
some special divine knowledge. Within this context Jesus
is presented as a mystical figure who communicates this
knowledge which saves. Both Docetism and Gnosticism end
up denying the humanity of Jesus. In opposition to this
type of thinking Ignatius of Antioch (d. 110 A.D.) pointed
out that the reality of salvation depended upon the reality
of the humanity of Jesus. If Jesus does not share the same
humanity as the rest of mankind then he cannot be regarded as the Saviour. On the other side there were those
who played down the divinity of Jesus in different ways.
Some reduced Jesus to a unique moral figure who inspired
people (*Moralism*). Others saw Jesus simply as a good man
who was subsequently adopted as the Son of God (Adoptionism). The principal spokesman against this outlook was
Ireneus (d. ca. 200 A.D.), Bishop of Lyons. He argued
that once the divinity of Jesus is ruled out then the reality
of salvation is also eliminated. Jesus must have been divine
if he is to be our Saviour.

The underlying issue common to most questions at this stage was how to reconcile the acceptance of the man Jesus as divine with belief in the oneness of God. To answer this question the Christian apologists tried to expand upon their insight into Jesus as the key to the presence of God in history and in the universe. They claimed that God had a power or energy within himself. This power or energy was the Word which separated itself from God and showed itself in the man Jesus. Within this scheme Jesus is presented as a type of semi-god who is subordinated to the absoluteness of the one God. Tertullian (d. 220 A.D.) takes up this subordinationist perspective, enlarges upon it, and in doing so provides a new terminology which was to have lasting influence upon christology. Tertullian speaks about Jesus as one person in whom there exist two substances which are not confused but conjoined. Not unlike Tertullian was Origen (d. 253 A.D.) who began by stressing the oneness of God in whom existed the Word as a mediating organ lower in rank than God the Father. It was this mediating principle, claimed Origen, that appears in Jesus.

Following Origen was Paul of Samosata who became Bishop of Antioch in 270 A.D. Paul, who is strongly anti-Origenist, sets out to safeguard the humanity of Jesus. He ends up by weakening the bond between Jesus and God. He sees the Word as "of one substance" (*homoousios*) with the Father in the sense of manifesting the same person of the Father but not having the same nature. He was condemned at the Synod of Antioch in 268 A.D. for his views, including his use of the expression "of one substance" His ideas were to reappear later in Nestorius and in the different christologies from Antioch.[6]

The next important figure to appear was Arius (d. 336 A.D.) who was a presbyter from Alexandria. According to Arius the Word/*Logos* is a creature, made out of nothing, so that there was a time when the Word did not exist. Yet the Word is prior to our temporal existence.

As such the Word is a semi-divine power which exists in the soul of Jesus. The overall effect of Arius was to make Jesus into a half-god somewhat like the hero gods of the ancient world (e.g. Olympus). As a result the divinity of Jesus is called into question at a fundamental level and his real humanity is also endangered.

The views of Arius and his supporters were condemned at the Council of Nicea in 325 A.D. Although primarily a Trinitarian Council, Nicea also provided a basic doctrinal point of departure for future christological discussions. In opposition to Arius it asserted that Jesus Christ is of one substance with the Father (*homoousios*). Equally anti-Arian it also declared : "Those who say there was a time when he was not . . . or was made out of nothing . . . are condemned by the Catholic Church."[7] The basic point for christology coming from Nicea was the clear assertion that Jesus Christ is fully divine, of one substance with God the Father. This put an end to the possibility of seeing Jesus simply as a god alongside the other pagan gods. It also eliminated any suggestion that the Word in Jesus was simply an emanation from God.[8] Most of all it provided a fixed point in a world of doctrinal giddiness.[9] From now on christological discussion would centre around the doctrine that Jesus Christ was of one substance with the Father. The precise meaning of this formula in all its implications had to be worked out. If Jesus is of one being with the Father what about the role of his humanity? How could the Son who is of one substance with the Father be a real man at the same time?

Although Nicea provided a fixed point for future discussions it took over forty years for its doctrine to be commonly accepted. Some felt it had gone too far in its formula of the Son being of one substance with the Father. A resurgence of Arianism followed. The main spokesman and defender of the Council of Nicea was Athanasius (d. 373 A.D.) who eventually won the day.

The Alexandrian and Antiochene
schools of christology

In the aftermath of Nicea two distinct schools of christology emerged. On the one hand you had the Word-flesh (*Logos-Sarx*) approach coming out of Alexandria. Here the emphasis was on the divinity of Jesus with particular attention being given to the unity between the Word and the flesh in Jesus. In its extreme form the Word-flesh christology eliminated the presence of a human soul in Jesus. On the other hand there was the Word-man (*Logos-anthropos*) christology which came from Antioch. Within this scheme the emphasis is placed on the humanity without prejudice to the primacy of the divine Word in Jesus. This approach promoted a dualism in christology which was difficult to overcome.

An extreme example of the Alexandrian School can be found in Apollinaris (d. 390 A.D.) who set out to explain how the Word could become man in Jesus. He pointed out that the eternal Word joined itself to the flesh of Jesus to form a special union. This special union was such that it gave rise to an understanding of Jesus as "a heavenly man". The union between the Word and the flesh in Jesus took the place which the soul would normally occupy in man. In reply to Apollinaris it was pointed out that by denying the existence of a human soul in Jesus he was in effect denying the real manhood of Jesus. As a result, in opposition to Apollinaris a Roman Synod (365 A.D.) which was later to be ratified by an Antiochene Synod, wrote: "But if an incomplete man is taken on then our salvation is incomplete, because the entire man is not saved."[10] This important point, which became known as the soteriological principle, was invoked on different occasions by several Fathers as the basic safeguard for the humanity of Jesus.[11]

In contrast to this extreme there was the Antiochene Word-man christology. One of the champions of this school was Theodore of Mopsuestia (d. ca. 428 A.D.). In a deliberately anti-Arian and Apollinarian vein Theodore stresses the distinction between the humanity and divinity, pointing out that Jesus is "not only God, nor also only man, but he is by nature in both, God as well as man".[12] When it comes to explaining the union between the human and the divine Jesus, Theodore is more ambiguous. He uses expressions such as the Word "assuming", "adopting", and "indwelling" in the human nature of Jesus, all of which suggest a dualism. Yet he does refer to the God-man unity as a unity of one person. This term "person" which is so problematic in christology originally meant a mask whereby different individuals through a fiction were regarded as one. When introduced into the doctrine of the Trinity it was intended primarily to indicate the existence of a single independence. At this stage it is not clear in Theodore whether he means by person an independent reality or whether perhaps the old original sense of person remains which would mean that the Word and the man Jesus are *merely regarded* as one.[13] This latter view seems to be the more commonly accepted one and it confirms the impression of dualism in Theodore's christology.

The central question now in the Patristic debate is that of trying to work out the unity between the Word and the man in Jesus. Nestorius (d. ca. 451 A.D.), a pupil of Theodore and belonging to the Antiochene tradition, takes up this issue with intense interest. He insists on the two natures remaining unaltered and distinct in the union that exists between them in Jesus. His reason for this is that he wants to maintain that the Word was not involved in any change by becoming Incarnate while at the same time acknowledging that the man Jesus lived a fully human life. This point comes to a head-on collision when he refuses to accept that Mary is the Mother of God (*theotokos*). Instead Mary is the Mother of Christ (*christotokos*). Consequently not only do you have the dualism of two distinct natures but also two persons in the sense that each nature has its own concrete individual existence (*prosopon*). The union for Nestorius between the two natures is merely a moral union.

At this point Cyril the Patriarch of Alexandria (d. 444 A.D.) enters the debate. He takes issue with Nestorius, asking him by letter to retreat from his teaching especially in regard to Mary. Nestorius replies coldly and ignores the request. A second letter from Cyril follows in which he draws up a commentary on the Council of Nicea and warns Nestorius to take note. Again Nestorius replies, this time pointing out that Cyril has not really understood what Nicea was saying. Both appeal to Rome. The outcome is the summoning of an ecumenical Council at Ephesus in 431 A.D. This Council condemns Nestorius and accepts the teaching of Cyril as laid out in his second letter to Nestorius which is now taken as the authoritative faith of the assembly. The condemnation of Nestorius is directed against his refusal to accept that the eternal Son of God was born of the virgin, suffered, died and rose again. Implicit in this is also a condemnation of his refusal to call Mary the Mother of God and to acknowledge the communication of divine and human properties in the one person of Jesus (known as the *communicatio idiomatum*). Acceptance of Cyril's second letter involved a recognition of the fact that the unity of the Word made flesh in Jesus is not simply a habitation, a relation, or the assumption of a man. Rather it is a "hypostatic union" or a "physical union". The overall contribution of the Council of Ephesus to christology was its affirmation of a real unity between the eternal Word and the man Jesus.[14]

Because Ephesus was so closely associated with Cyril of Alexandria it provoked considerable opposition from the Antiochenes. This opposition was led by John of Antioch (d. 441 A.D.) and was based on the ambiguity of Cyril's terminology, especially his reference to the unity between the Word and the flesh as a unity "of one nature". For the Antiochenes the scent of Appollinaris seemed to be surfacing once again. In an effort to overcome this recurring conflict between the Alexandrians and the Antiochenes an "Edict of Union" was drawn up in 433 A.D. between Cyril of Alexandria and John of Antioch. This document, directed towards doctrinal reconciliation, acknowledged the Antiochene claim of two distinct and complete natures in Jesus Christ while at the same time recognising the Alexandrian concern for the unity of person in Jesus and the right for Mary to be called the Mother of God.

However laudable, this agreed statement did not keep the warring factions apart. Some of the Antiochenes continued to reject Cyril of Alexandria. These became known as Nestorians. Extremists from the other side persisted in an exaggerated unitarian christology giving rise to the heresy known as Monophysitism. This heresy held that there was only one nature in Jesus Christ and that this was a divine nature. One such extremist was Eutyches (d. 454 A.D.) who took upon himself the task of wiping out all traces of Nestorianism. In doing so he fastened upon certain formulae of Cyril without fully understanding them, and then quite often it was the more ambiguous formulae of Cyril such as the union "in one nature". Eutyches goes so far in his fanaticism that he denies the existence of a full human nature in Jesus. One of the many difficulties here between the Nestorians and the Monophysites is that of language. To be sure Cyril had used the formula "of one nature in Christ" but he had done so with the intention of safeguarding the unity of two natures in Jesus.

Flavian (d. 449 A.D.) of Constantinople recognises this growing confusion over terminology. He convenes a local Synod at Constantinople and condemns Eutyches. Flavian points out that after the Word became flesh there existed in Christ "two natures in one hypostasis and in one person". For the first time the pairing of the words "person" and "hypostasis" has been introduced. This removes the suspicion that the term person as applied to Jesus Christ could imply the realities of God and Man as if they were one in the way a group functions as one. This qualification of person by hypostasis drove home that the person of the Incarnation was the one eternal Word of God.

This condemnation was ratified by Pope Leo the Great (d. 461 A.D.) who also forwarded a lengthy and important document to Flavian in which he laid out the doctrine of Jesus Christ (*Tomus ad Flavium* 449 A.D.). Amongst other things Leo spoke out clearly about the existence "of two natures and their properties . . . being united in one person . . . so that one and the same Jesus Christ might on the one hand die and on the other be immortal".[15]

In spite of these positive contributions from Constantinople and Rome Eutyches persists in his stubborn ways. In pursuit of his own position he "manages" a hearing before an assembly of Bishops at Ephesus through the Emperor Theodosius II in 449 A.D. In the chair was Dioscurus, patriarch of Alexandria and successor to Cyril, who intimidated the bishops into declaring Eutyches to be orthodox and condemning Flavian.

The Council of Chalcedon

At this stage not only was the confusion compounded but serious divisions within the Church seemed imminent. To counteract this alarming state of affairs Marcion, the new Emperor, in consultation with the Pope called a general council of the Church at Chalcedon in 451 A.D. It was attended by six hundred bishops, three Papal Legates, and two representatives from Latin Africa. This made it not only the largest christological council but also the most important in the history of Christianity. The first business on the agenda was an examination of the legality of the assembly at Ephesus in 499 A.D. known as the "Robber

Synod", and its proceedings. The outcome of this was a condemnation of the scheming Dioscurus and a nullification of the treatment of Flavian by Eutyches.

Attention was then focused upon the christological issue. A commission was appointed and a scheme was drawn up. The language of this scheme was compromising and ambiguous. The Papal Legates protested and threatened to move the Council to Italy. A new commission was set up and they formulated a confession of christological faith acceptable to all. The sources employed in this confession were the Council of Nicea, Cyril's second letter to Nestorius, the Edict of Union, the contribution of Flavian at Constantinople, and the Tome of Pope Leo the Great. The formal definition ran as follows:

> In imitation of the Holy Fathers we confess with one voice that our Lord Jesus Christ is one and the same Son . . .; the same perfect in his divinity and the same perfect in his humanity;
>
> Truly God and the same truly man of a rational soul and a body;
>
> Of one nature with the Father according to the divinity and the same of one nature with us according to the humanity in all things like us except in sin;
>
> Before the ages begotten of the Father according to the divinity but the same in the last days for us and for our salvation born according to the humanity of Mary the Virgin and Mother of God;
>
> One and the same Christ, Lord, only begotten, in two natures;
>
> Without confusion, without change, without division and without separation.
>
> The difference of the natures is not removed through the union but, rather, the property of each nature is

preserved and they coalesce in one person (*prosopon*)
and one indepenaence (*hypostasis*);

Not divided or separated into two persons,

But one and the same only begotten Son, God-Word
Jesus Christ the Lord."[16]

Chalcedon was a Council of synthesis. It brought together for the first time all the different insights that had
accumulated over the last couple of centuries of debate. It
incorporated the best traditions of both the Alexandrian
and the Antiochene schools, emphasising the reality of
the two natures existing in one and the same person. It
countered the possibilities of any misunderstanding that
might have attached to the Councils of Nicea and
Ephesus. It balanced the Nicean formula of "one substance with the Father" with the assertion of "one substance with us according to humanity" and checked the
hypostatic unity of Ephesus by recognising the reality of the
human nature in Jesus. Most of all it laid down the terms
of reference in which the mystery of Jesus Christ should
be discussed, namely that of substance, nature and person.
On the other hand it is important to realise the limits
of Chalcedon. It did not offer or pretend to offer a solution
to the different christological questions that had been
raised by Apollinarianism, Nestorianism, and Monophysitism. Instead it provided the bricks and mortar that
might be used in the construction of an answer to these
questions. Even then the precise shape and colour of these
Chalcedonian bricks were not always clear. It did however distinguish between nature and person, which was a
helpful advance. It used the idea of nature to get across
the human and the divine dimensions in Jesus Christ
whereas the idea of person was linked by Chalcedon with
hypostasis thereby indicating the concrete singular individuality of Jesus. These distinctions, though helpful,
were by no means exhaustive. Nuances of meaning had yet

to be ironed out. To this extent Chalcedon was only a beginning[17] though unfortunately in later centuries it was seen as an end in itself.

In spite of this timely synthesis by Chalcedon, christological controversy continued for some time. A division which had been threatening for many years between the east and the west arose on the basis of Chalcedon. The west adhered to Chalcedon whereas the east either rejected it or veered towards a Monophysite interpretation of it. This Monophysite stream explicitly rejected the two nature formula of Chalcedon and adopted an extreme form of Cyrillian christology.

An attempt at reconciliation was initiated under the Emperor Justinian (d. 565 A.D.). The leading figure here was Leontius of Byzantium who was a monastic theologian. Leontius came up with a theory which said that the human nature of Jesus is in the hypostasis of the divine Word. This meant that the human nature was *en-hypostatic* as distinct from the impression given by Apollinarius and continued by Cyril to some extent that the human nature had no hypostasis thus implying that it was an impersonal *an-hypostatic* human nature. This potentially helpful suggestion of Leontius, however, was taken up by the Monophysites and inverted to promote their own cause of denying two natures in Christ. From here Monophysitism developed into the logical conclusion of Monothelitism—a view which held that there was only one will, a divine will, in Jesus.

Orthodox theologians of the seventh century, however, recognised the betrayal of Chalcedon which lurked behind this formula of one will in Jesus. As a result the third Council of Constantinople (680-681 A.D.) not only endorsed Chalcedon but also explicitly affirmed the existence of two wills and operations—human and divine— in Jesus. As such these two will exist not in opposition but rather in such a way that the "human will" follows and responds to the "divine will". This doctrine of Con-

stantinople was merely a drawing out of the full implications of Chalcedon. It was important for the Church to
highlight the reality of Christ's human will if it were to
remain faithful to the Patristic principle of soteriology
which says "what is not assumed is not saved". Further
it was even more important for the Church at this stage
to point towards the existence of a human will if the
reality of Christ's personalised humanity was to survive
the assaults of Monophysitism.

In retrospect it must be admitted that Chalcedon
saved the human side of the mystery of Jesus Christ in
western theology. On several occasions, whether through
Apollinarianism, Eutychianism, Monophysitism, or Monothelitism, the human side of Jesus Christ was on the verge
of being swallowed up by the divine nature. To this extent
Chalcedon stands out as a normative christological land-
mark. It provides us with a balanced formulation of the
universal significance of the Christ-Event, a formulation
that needs to be constantly interpreted and re-interpreted
according to the Spirit-filled experience of the Christian
community.

8 Reshaping the christological dogma

The christological dogma of Chalcedon has been more or less universally accepted down through the centuries. The acceptance of the dogma took place within the framework of the Aristotelian categories of person, nature and substance as adopted by Chalcedon. This framework in turn was further refined by Scholastic Philosophy, especially under the influence of Thomism. The Aristotelian-Thomistic framework has served and safeguarded most successfully the substance of the christological dogma for many centuries. In recent times, however, there has been a growing disenchantment with the traditional formulation of Chalcedon. In this chapter we will examine some of the contemporary criticisms of Chalcedon. We will then try in the light of these criticisms to relocate the doctrine of Chalcedon within a different frame of reference. Lastly we will explain this relocation of Chalcedon through the aid of anthropology.

Chalcedon in contemporary thought

Uneasiness with the traditional formulation of Chalcedon only seriously crept into theology in the nineteenth century. The tone of this uneasiness within the Protestant tradition was set by Frederick Schleiermacher (d. 1834) who undertook a critical examination of the language of Chalcedon.[1] This criticism was sharpened by the rise of biblical research and its application to the person of Jesus in the New Testament during the nineteenth and twentieth centuries. Within Catholic circles criticism of Chalcedon has become a reality since the fifteenth anniversary of the Council in 1951.[2] The underlying object of these criticisms within the Catholic and Protestant traditions is the language of the Aristotelian-Thomistic framework. It is pointed out that the language of this particular philosophical framework no longer enjoys the privileged position it possessed in the past. There has emerged a plurality of philosophical frameworks —analytical, existential, personalist, phenomenological, processive and structuralist—which add and subtract in their own way to both the meaning and content of traditional christology. Consequently a definite shift in meaning has taken place concerning the technical terms of Chalcedon as supported in the past by the Aristotelian-Thomistic framework. The traditional import of words like substance, person, and nature, has changed within this transition from philosophical uniformity to pluriformity.

The issue at stake here is not the doctrinal truth of Chalcedon which is highly respected. Nor is the issue here the validity or non-validity of the Aristotelian-Thomistic philosophy in itself which is a separate matter quite independent of christology. Rather the basic question being raised is whether the Aristotelian-Thomistic framework can continue to serve the substance of Chalcedon, in virtue of the fact that the meaning of its primary terms of reference has changed fundamentally in this century. The urgency of this question will become apparent by briefly examining the shift in meaning concerning these primary terms of reference and some of the problems consequent upon this change in meaning.

The first primary and technical term of traditional christology which has undergone a basic change of meaning is that of "substance". The original meaning of this term was that of an underlying support for the different accidental qualities and appearances that a thing possessed. When Chalcedon, following Nicea, said Jesus was of one substance with the Father (*homoousios*) it intended to emphasise that there was an underlying identity as distinct from likeness (*homoiousios*), imitation, representation or anything else between Jesus and God. The purpose therefore of this term was to get across the underlying identity and unity between Jesus and God. One could say crudely speaking that the Council was affirming that Jesus was "of the same stuff"[3] as God and man provided one understands "stuff" in the non-material underlying qualitative sense of that word.

In the twentieth century, however, the word substance has come to mean something quite different. It refers to undifferentiated raw material which presents itself externally for man's manipulation. As such, substance is understood as a purely physical quantified reality. When this modern understanding of substance is applied to Jesus, as of one substance with the Father, the impression is conveyed that Jesus is made out of the same lump of divine material as the Father in much the same way that two loaves of bread are made out of the same lump of dough and can therefore be said to be of the same substance.[4] However, the underlying identity and unity between Jesus and God is not intended to be a physical quantified material identity. Rather it was an underlying identity of origin and relationship between Jesus and God. This identity was a living, dynamic, and qualitative identity as distinct from a static, physical, and quantitative identity which is falsely implied in the contemporary understanding of substance.

This distortion becomes even more grotesque when one asserts, as one must, following Chalcedon, that Jesus is of one substance in regard to man and God. Here the impression is given that Jesus is some kind of double-layered static reality composed of two different kinds of physical material, lying alongside each other somewhat like oil and water. In this case the image of a divided Jesus dualistically composed of distinct pieces or blocks of divinity and humanity is unavoidable. This of course is quite contrary to the original intention of Chalcedon and raises serious questions about the usefulness of the traditional category of substance for communicating the underlying identity between Jesus and God and man. The seriousness of this question has already been felt and anticipated to some extent in English-speaking liturgical circles. A recent English translation of the Nicean Creed has changed the wording "consubstantial with the Father" to "one in being with the Father" as a more effective way to express the profound unity between Father and Son.[5] This change alone indicates the ambiguity attached to the word substance in contemporary thought. The same ambiguity has also been experienced in this century within eucharistic theology which depended so much in the past on the category of substance.[6]

The next set of primary and technical terms in traditional christology whose meaning has changed is that of nature and person. When these terms were first used by Chalcedon there was still a certain ambiguity surrounding their meaning. With time however they received a more definite meaning under the influence of Aristotelian-Thomistic philosophy. It is this received meaning of the two nature—one person model that we are primarily interested in here. For traditional christology person was defined as "the individual substance of a rational nature".[7] Following this definition person was understood to refer to that which gives concrete individual existence to a rational nature. As such, the word person embraces a centre of unity belonging to the bearer of individuality.[8] As the centre of unity and bearer of individuality the person does not act nor is the person conscious of any particular activity. Instead person in traditional christology is used in an ontological sense referring to the individual "who" or subject of a particular concrete existence. This ontological concept of person exists in complete contrast to the modern understanding of person which is informed primarily by psychology.

In contemporary usage the word person refers to the ego or the self as conscious of itself in relationship to other people and the world around it. It is the person who is the source of freedom, activity, self-consciousness, and responsibility. As such it is the person who is the centre of experience and who directs the movements of the individual in response to these experiences. These two meanings of the word person—ontological and psychological—are quite different and create serious difficulties in trying to understand the meaning of Chalcedon.

Turning to the idea of nature in traditional christology we discover that nature is the source of activity. In man, for example, it is the human nature which thinks, understands, and is conscious of itself. Nature is the principle of operation and the operations of a nature are attributed to a non-acting person as the centre and bearer of individuality. On the other hand, however, nature today refers to some abstract quality which attaches itself to the reality under consideration. In the case of a human nature this abstract quality is known as human-ness which belongs to the acting of an individual human being. Furthermore it is this quality or characteristic which makes an individual the particular kind of individual he is and so differentiates him from other individuals.

This necessarily brief analysis of the terms of the two nature—one person model clearly indicates that a complete change of meaning has taken place concerning the primary terms of traditional christology. What was formerly called person now approximates to what we call nature and what was known as nature in the past is understood today as person.[9] Failure to recognise this change in meaning tends to create confusion in the mind of modern man when he tries to understand the Chalcedonian formula. Examples of such confusion can be seen by looking at the traditional statement that in Jesus there are two natures which exist in one divine person.

The expression "one divine person" today is understood in a purely psychological sense as if in Jesus there was only one psychological person and that this one psychological person is an exclusively divine person. This misinterpretation of the expression "one divine person" in turn is taken to exclude the possibility of seeing Jesus as a real human person in the psychological sense of that word. As a result the human nature of Jesus tends to become depersonalised and is reduced to the level of a mere passive instrument which is subordinated to the movements of the one divine person (psychological). In reality, however, the affirmation by Chalcedon of a human nature alongside a divine nature must of necessity include an understanding of Jesus as a human person in the psychological sense.[10] The end result of this confusion concerning the term person is the reproduction of a modern form of Monophysitism.

Another example of this kind of confusion that can occur in the two nature—one person model concerns the use of the concept nature. Quite often the word nature is used univocally in reference to the humanity and divinity as if to imply that one is talking about the same kind of reality in both instances.[11] The underlying assumption here is that there is a one-to-one correspondence between the human and the divine nature in Jesus which is of course quite false. As a result discussion of the divine and the human in Jesus takes place as if they were numerically and quantitatively the same kind of entities. This divine-human equation in turn leads to an irremovable form of Nestorian dualism within the two nature—one person model.

This analysis of the change in meaning of the primary terms of Chalcedon and the confusion which can occur from this change suggests that there is a real need for caution in present-day discussions of christology within the traditional framework. Whether in the light of these changes it is possible for the Aristotelian-Thomistic framework to continue safeguarding the dogma of Chalcedon for modern man is a question that we must leave open here.

One possible way of overcoming the hazards which

we have met with by the language of the traditional frame of reference is to relocate the doctrine of Chalcedon within categories which are less philosophically determined than those of substance, person, and nature. In order to do this in a way that is faithful to the defined dogma it is necessary first of all to extricate the doctrinal truth and meaning of Chalcedon from the terms substance, person, and nature.

Briefly the burden of the expression "of one substance with the Father according to divinity and the same of one substance with us according to humanity" is to get across the identity as distinct from likeness of Jesus with God and man. To this extent Jesus is equally one with God and man. Following on this the meaning of the two nature—one person model takes this truth a little further. It suggests that the mystery of Jesus Christ is a mystery of unity within distinction. There is absolute unity of person in the ontological sense of a single existent reality that forms a divine centre of unity in which the human and the divine inhere. This divine centre of unity in Jesus is as much constituted by his humanity as it is by his divinity. The divine ontological person is that which results from the coming together of the divine and the human in Jesus as well as that which holds in existence the divine and the human. This divine personal centre of unity is what has been traditionally called the hypostatic union of the divine and the human in Jesus. As such this unique union in Jesus is identified with the divine person (*hypostasis*) of the *Logos*. It is this reality of a single divine person which represents the side of unity within the mystery of Jesus.

On the other hand there is within this ontological unity a distinction of natures which exist without confusion, without change, without division, and without separation. This means that the distinction of natures is not a distinction of dichotomy which would produce as is too often the case a type of rival dualism between the two natures. Instead the distinction of natures is a distinction of involvement between the human and the divine, between God and man, without however confusing or diminishing the distinctiveness of these two realities.[12] The human nature in Jesus is so real that it must include a full human person in the psychological sense of that word as its support.[13] If this were not the case the humanity of Jesus would be just a mere impersonal abstraction. As for the divine nature one must be more careful here since we are dealing with a reality belonging to a different order of being in comparison to that of the human nature. The divine nature is best understood as a real distinct dimension in Jesus which may if necessary be described as a divine person in the psychological sense provided we remember that we use the word person here analogously and not properly speaking. This duality of natures in Jesus implies that we acknowledge the existence of a human psychological centre of self-consciousness involved in and related to a divine psychological centre of self-consciousness within the one ontological person of Jesus.[14] This particular truth is demanded by Chalcedon in its affirmation, directed against Monophysitism, of a real human and divine nature within the one person of Jesus. This interpretation of Chalcedon is confirmed by the council of Constantinople which explicitly rejects Monothelitism. Furthermore the same point is reaffirmed in the encyclical, *Sempiternus Rex,* of Pius XII in 1951 which refused to condemn as erroneous the view which stated that there were two psychological subjects in the one ontological person of Jesus.[15]

In other words to put the matter as simply as possible the two nature—one person model of Chalcedon means that in Jesus there is a fully human centre of self-consciousness and a divine centre of self-consciousness which are hypostatically united in one divine person. As such the council of Chalcedon was trying to explain the mystery of God and man as really united in Jesus through the concepts of substance, nature and person. It is precisely at this level of a real unity between God and man that the full mystery of Jesus Christ must be stated and it is at this level that

we propose to relocate the doctrinal truth of Chalcedon
for today.

Jesus as true God and true man

In our analysis of the meaning of Chalcedon the two basic
terms of reference which kept cropping up were God and
man. No matter how one explains the christological dogma
reference must be made to the reality of God and the reality
of man as united in Jesus. The underlying truth therefore
of Chalcedon is the simple though profound statement that
the reality of Jesus is true God and true man. Indeed
Chalcedon itself refers explicitly to Jesus as true God
and true man before introducing the technical terms of
substance, person, and nature. It is this formulation of
the mystery of Christ which must be explored if we are
to communicate the universal significance of the Christ-
Event in a world which no longer appreciates the technical
terms of traditional christology.

This relocation and reformulation of Chalcedon has
definite advantages. It situates the mystery of Jesus Christ
where it truly belongs, namely within a perspective which
refers to both God and man. Further it puts christology
into a frame of reference that can accommodate itself to
the changing philosophical moods of the day. Adopting
this formula, then, the question arises: How can we say
with all due regard for the single reality of Jesus that he
is true God and true man at one and the same time?
To answer this question we must go back further to the
epistemological roots of the claim that Jesus is true God
and true man. How did the apostles and the Church come
to know Jesus as true God and true man? What is the
basis in experience and understanding of this statement?
How can we today continue to credibly make this extraordinary claim for the founder of Christianity?

To answer these questions we must invoke a basic
theological principle which has been lost sight of in tradi-

tional christology. This principle may be formulated in the following way. God cannot be encountered "over" or "above", "beyond" or "beneath" one's encounter with reality.[16] Man's experience of God does not normally take place on a vertical or a one-to-one basis.[17] Rather man can only experience God in and through the finite medium of the world in which he lives.[18] Conversely, God communicates himself to man in and through the finite medium of created reality. Part and parcel of this created reality through which God mediates himself is the created reality of humanity.

This basic principle is an intrinsic component of the Judaeo–Christian tradition. In Judaism God was understood as the reality which works in and through history, in and through the history of the people, a nation, and the prophets of that nation. Within Christianity God shows himself in and through the life, death, and resurrection of Jesus. St John tells us explicitly that no man has ever seen God directly (*Jn 1:18*). St Thomas at a later stage reminds us vividly that God cannot be known in his essence by man since the nature of man's knowledge is restricted by the mode of his knowing which in this life takes place through finite reality.[19] Ultimately of course the truth of this theological principle rests upon the foundations of cognitional theory and epistemology. All knowledge and understanding including knowledge and understanding of God, is derived from man's experience of the world in which he lives. There has been a tendency at times to imagine that knowledge and understanding of life, especially when it concerns God, takes place in some rarified region of man's mind in isolation from his ordinary everyday experience. In fact, however, such knowledge and understanding of life and of God is always rooted in man's multiple experiences of the world around him. Similarly our knowledge and understanding of the divinity of Jesus can only take place in and through the humanity of Jesus.[20]

Accepting this basic theological principle and applying it to the mystery of Jesus Christ we can begin to explain how Jesus is known to be true God and true man
without sacrificing the unity of this mystery. The reality
of God in Jesus is a reality mediated in and through the
manhood of Jesus. This means in effect that God in Jesus
is revealed not as something "over" or "above", "beyond"
or "beneath" his humanity but rather as a reality within
his manhood. In other words the divinity of Jesus is a
distinct dimension perceptible in and through his humanity. The mystery lies neither beyond nor beneath the man
Jesus but rather in his being the particular type of man
he was. The divine remains what it is as Chalcedon says
without confusion and without change while being per-
ceived as such in the measure of his humanity from
which it is not divided or separated.[21]

As we have already pointed out in our analysis of
the meaning of Chalcedon the distinction between the
human and the divine in Jesus is a distinction of involvement between two realities and not a distinction of dichotomy. This distinction of involvement between the human
and the divine Jesus mirrors the more general distinction
of involvement that exists between God and the world at
large. God and the universe in their respective distinctiveness are closely involved without being confused. This
involvement reaches its fulfilment in Jesus in such a way
that the distinct integrity of God and man remains.[22]

Consequently the involvement of God and man in
Jesus should not be thought of as a synthesis or a mixture
or some hybrid-reality resulting from a combination of
the human and the divine.[23] Each of these combinations is
ruled out by the Chalcedonian clause "without confusion
and without change, without division and without separation". The unity between God and man in Jesus is much
more real and intensive than such a synthesis mixture or
hybrid-reality. It is a unity which is so real, comprehensive and inclusive that we can justifiably say in all truth

that Jesus is true God and true man as a single assertion about the one reality of Jesus. It was precisely this point concerning the reality of the unity between Jesus and God that the doctrine of the hypostatic union was trying to preserve and communicate.

It is equally important to realise that the divinity of Jesus is not a second substance over and above his humanity. We do not have in the mystery of Jesus Christ a man called Jesus in whom is realised the presence of God as something extrinsically distinct from his being man. If this were the case it would be difficult to see what saving significance such divinity could have in the light of the Patristic principle "what God has not assumed is not redeemed". Instead the man Jesus precisely in his particular humanity is the presence of God. The revelation of God to man takes place "in the humanity of Jesus",[24] and not outside his humanity. To deny the reality of this mediating role of the humanity of Jesus would be to lapse into a form of Docetism. It will be noticed that in this analysis of the formula "Jesus is true God and true man" the emphasis has been put on the humanity of Jesus. This is necessarily the case in virtue of the fact that God chose the created humanity of Jesus in and through which to reveal himself. It is the mystery of God that is being revealed and the agency of this revelation is the humanity of Jesus. Within the mystery of Jesus as true God and true man we do not understand what it is to be God nor indeed do we fully understand what it is to be man. Less still do we understand what it is to be God and man at one and the same time.[25] However, in so far as we do have some experience and understanding of what it is to be man we can begin to glimpse the mystery of God in and through the man Jesus. It is this Jesus, who was known as a man and confessed to be the Son of God in humanity, that now opens up the mystery of God. The only mode of access we have to the divine Sonship of Jesus is in and through his humanity. We can know nothing about the divinity of

Jesus apart from his humanity. For this reason the basic emphasis must be on his humanity and it is only therefore by trying to understand this humanity that we will ever reach an understanding of his divinity.

This emphasis on the humanity implies that the divinity of Jesus can only be fully discovered in the perfection of his humanity. In fact the divinity of Jesus is disclosed through the perfection of his humani:,.[26] This means in effect that Jesus is known to be divine in and through the fullness of his humanity. By being perfect man in all that this implies Jesus manifested through his life, death and resurrection that he was God in human form. In realising the fullness of his humanity in all its graced capacities Jesus revealed the presence of the divine within the heart of man. Only those "who forget the essence of man is unbounded will find it difficult to accept that there was a man who being man in the fullest sense is God's existence in the world".[27] It is only in and through an appreciation of "the perfection of humanity" that we "will be able to acknowledge the mystery of his divinity".[28] It is the implications of this emphasis on the humanity of Jesus that we must now take up and try to explain in more detail.

From anthropology to christology

How can Jesus be known to be true God by being true man? What does it mean to say that Jesus is discovered to be divine through his humanity? To what extent can humanity mediate divinity? In what way does the perfection of humanity incorporate divinity? It will be noticed that basically these questions are anthropological in character. They ask about the nature of man and in particular about the nature of the man Jesus. To this extent anthropology is the key to christology;[29] it opens up the meaning of Jesus as true God and true man. This can

be seen by examining the biblical and theological understanding of man.

Beginning with the biblical doctrine of man. we are
told that man was made in the image and likeness of God
(*Gen 1:26-27*). In the light of evolution we know that
this implies more that man was graced with a capacity to
mirror the image and likeness of God, than that he
actually realised this image and likeness of God. Man
from the beginning was called to communion with God,
a communion that would reflect the image and likeness of
God within his being. As called he "was a type of the one
who was to come" (*Rom 5:14*). On the other hand, however, we know that this gratuitous calling is rejected by
man from the beginning. The graced capacity within the
heart of man to reflect the image and likeness of God is
thwarted and frustrated by the reality of sin (*Gen 3*).
Sin is a turning away of the creature from the creator;
it is a separation of man from God; it is a rejection by
man of the gratuitous calling implanted in the depths of
his being to communion with God. In a word "sin is the
refusal by man to share in the divine nature".[30]

It is against this background that Jesus appears as a
man among men, not just another man among men but
as a man of God among men. Jesus emerges historically
as one who is very closely involved with God and as one
whose life is centred around the mystery of God. He
announces the Kingdom of God and intimates the presence
of a filial relationship between himself as Son and God as
Father. Throughout the life, death and resurrection there
is a closeness, nearness, and intimacy between Jesus and
God. This fact allows us to talk about the existence of
an underlying communion between Jesus and God, a
communion which is later interpreted ontologically as the
hypostatic union between God and man. In the light of
this communion with God Jesus is understood as the one
who restores the image and likeness of God that had been
obscured from the beginning by man through sin. The

image and likeness of God implanted in the heart of man from the beginning as a grace and a calling to be realised is now perfectly embodied for the first time in Jesus, who realises full hypostatic communion with God.

One of the most powerful expressions of this underlying communion between Jesus and God is that of the doctrine of the sinlessness of Jesus (*Jn 8:46, 14:30; 2 Cor 5:21; 1 Pet 2:22; Heb 4:15*). This doctrine of the sinlessness of Jesus should not be understood merely as the absence of moral lapses, human offences, or personal transgression within the life of Jesus which are only external symptoms of sin.[31] Rather the sinlessness of Jesus is a much more deeply rooted reality which is based on the fundamental fact that there was no separation from God in the life of Jesus. Put more positively the sinlessness of Jesus is derived from the radically theocentric attitude of his whole life through which he is determined to respond to the grace and calling to communion with God. Further, the sinlessness should not be presented monophysitically as if the man Jesus did not genuinely experience the temptations of sin. Such a picture would be a denial of the historically reliable accounts of the temptations in the desert (*Mk 2:12ff; Lk 4:2ff; Mt 4:1ff*). The truth here is not that the man Jesus was not able to sin (*non posse peccare*) but that the man Jesus was able not to sin (*posse non peccare*) just as we are able with our freedom to sin or not to sin.[32] In other words the sinlessness of Jesus should not be conceived of in terms of an *a priori* projection of impeccability in a way that would destroy the reality of his humanity. The New Testament never says that Jesus could not sin; it states rather that Jesus in fact did not sin.[33] The sinlessness of Jesus, therefore, should be understood as the achievement of a rich response by the man Jesus to the gift of God's grace throughout his life.[34]

By maintaining an unbroken bond of hypostatic union with God Jesus realised the graced capacity of his

humanity for communion with God. In doing so he revealed the image and likeness of God within the heart of
man. It is in this sense that we can say that the perfection
of his humanity through communion with God mediates
divinity and so suggest that Jesus is known to reflect the
image of God by being true man and that therefore his
divinity is disclosed through the fullness of his humanity.
This does not mean that the sinlessness of Jesus is his
divinity. Rather the sinlessness of Jesus is an expression, a
negative one at that, of his communion with God which is
the basis of his humanity revealing his divinity.

Traces of this type of thinking about Jesus manifesting
the in-built image of God in his humanity as a result of
his communion with God can be found in the New Testament literature. One of its clearest expressions is to be
found in the letter to the Hebrews which points out that
Jesus "reflects the glory of God and bears the very stamp
of his nature upholding the universe by his word and
power" (*Heb 1:3*). According to the exegetes the language
of this verse refers back to the biblical account of the
creation of man. To be the stamp of God's being is to be
in his image. Further, ideas like "reflection" and "glory"
are often used in the scriptures to describe the mirror
relationship of similarity that exists between a son and
his father.[35] Thus Jesus stands in an imaging relationship
to God in the same way as any true son images his father.
Jesus does this as a real Son by being in communion with
God his Father and can therefore truly reflect the image of
God in his humanity.

Again the same kind of thinking is found in Philip-
pians chapter two which talks of Jesus "in the form of God
. . . being born in the likeness of man" (*Phil 2:6-7*). Here
too the exegetes tell us that the idea of Jesus "in the form
of God" goes back to the Genesis account of man being
made in the image and likeness of God (*Gen 1:26*).[36]
A similar and more explicit echo of this is found in the

letter to the Colossians which directly calls Jesus "the image of the invisible God" (*Col 1:15*).

Within this context it is interesting to note that the Second Vatican Council, in so far as it discusses the relationship between Jesus and God, also employs these biblical categories. It too sees Jesus as the "new man" and the "final Adam" who "restores the divine likeness which had been disfigured from the first sin onwards".[37] This restoration of the divine image and likeness of God takes place in the man Jesus through his communion with God. In this way we see how the biblical understanding of man helps us to appreciate how the humanity of Jesus could disclose divinity. It was in and through the communion of Jesus with God that the perfection of his humanity took place and so therefore he could truly mirror the image and likeness of God in his being. Jesus is the image of the invisible God because he is in full hypostatic communion with God.

It is as well to note at this stage that the biblical expression "Jesus is the image of the invisible God" is probably one of the more accurate ways theologically speaking of expressing the divinity of Jesus. It is in direct contrast to the more ambiguous though frequently used expression "Jesus is God". This latter formula if understood according to the normal usage of the English copula "is" is open to monophysitic misinterpretation. It suggests an identification between the subject "Jesus" and the predicate "God" along the lines that the subject "Peter" is identical with the predicate "man" in the sentence "Peter is a man". In fact however this type of identification between Jesus and God is open to confusion.[38] On the one hand it offends against the absolute transcendence of God in himself who dwells in light inaccessible and on the other hand it destroys the mystery of Jesus Christ as the historical revelation of God. It is important to distinguish here between the revelation of a reality and the reality itself, or more accurately between the expression of a reality and the reality itself.

The expression of a reality especially through the historical revelation of that reality is not equivalent to the reality itself. If this were not so there would be no expression or revelation but rather pure naked reality. The mystery of Jesus Christ is the expression or revelation of God to man in historical form. The mystery of God however is not exhausted in Jesus. There can never be a total expression of God on the level of creation. The finite can never contain the totality of the infinite. The mystery of Jesus Christ is the key to the mystery of God. It must not, however, take away the mystery of God. In the light of these observations it is much more desirable to talk therefore about Jesus as the image of the invisible God than to talk simply about Jesus as God.

If one insists on the formula "Jesus is God" then one should complete the formula and say "Jesus is God *and* man" or "Jesus is God in human form". There is a fundamental difference between Jesus as God and Jesus as God and man just as there is a difference between God as God in himself and God as man in Jesus. Straight christological "is" statements when they refer to God must be qualified if we are to avoid misunderstanding and misinterpretation.[39] It is only through the mystery of Jesus Christ that we begin to glimpse the mystery of God and it is for that reason that Jesus as the image of God is one of the more helpful theological formulations of the divinity of Jesus. It cautions us against any simplistic identification of image with reality that in the end would destroy both image and reality. We must now turn to the theological understanding of man and see how this can illuminate the claim that Jesus is known to be divine in and through his humanity.

One of the most popular themes in theological anthropology today is that which talks about man as a self-transcending being. Man is understood as a being who is open to the world around him. Within this openness he reaches out beyond himself and the world in which he lives.[40] As such man has an unbounded capacity for self-transcendence. This unbounded capacity shows itself in man in a variety of ways such as the reality of a basic orientation in freedom and knowledge towards the supernatural,[41] the relentless existence of an unrestricted desire to know,[42] and the permanent presence of a quest for the unconditional in life.[43] In each case the goal of this endless seeking and searching through self-transcendence is the inexhaustible mystery we call God. The essence of man is a request for self-transcendence, a demand to rise above himself, to step outside his environment, and to enter into communion with God.[44] Yet it is this essence of man that cannot realise itself without the gracious initiative of God. Whatever description we give to man, therefore, reference must be made to God somewhere along the line if it is to be a complete description. One way or the other we can say that man is an *ascending self-transcending being* and that the inauguration as well as the terminus of this dynamic drive within the being of man is the mystery of God itself.

Because this understanding of man refers to God and because the other term in the mystery of Jesus Christ is God certain basic observations must also be made about the mystery of God. In making these observations it is important to remind ourselves about the real limitations that exist when it comes to talking about the mystery of God. Great care and caution must be exercised in our discourse so that we do not destroy the majesty and magnificence of God by reducing him to the level of a worldly reality. It is astonishing how lightly we manipulate the reality of God as though we were dealing with just another object alongside other finite objects. It is even more astonishing how overly objective our thinking about God tends to become as if we were in possession of some form of secret and absolute knowledge about God in himself and his particular movements. Both of these temptations must be avoided if we are to retain the credibility of God and the integrity of the mystery of Jesus Christ.

In so far as we accept the reality of God (and such pre-acceptance, no matter how primitive or private, is essential for a right understanding of the mystery of Jesus Christ) we can say that God is a self-communicating reality. The self-communication of God takes place primarily in and through the gift of creation and the grace of human existence. Arising out of our experience of the gift of creation and the grace of existence is born the acknowledgement of a depth dimension to life that can only be adequately explained by reference to that which we call God. In the light of these experiences we talk about God in an elementary sense as goodness and love. Goodness, as St Thomas tells us, is diffusive; it spreads itself out. Similarly love is a reality which is outgoing; it shares itself. To this extent we can talk about God as an outgoing and diffusive reality who is present in and through the world around us. In this sense we can begin to describe God as a *descending self-communicating being*.

If one stands back a little and looks at these basic descriptions of God and man one is struck by the fact that here we have two mutually attracting and complementary realities. There is an underlying magnetism between God as a self-communicating reality and man as a self-transcending being. When this attracting compatibility is placed in the historical context of God's dealings with mankind we can say that the reality of Jesus embodies *the* unique point of intrinsic contact between God's self-communication and man's self-transcendence. The ascending dynamic of man's unbounded spirit and the descending grace of God's presence in the world reaches an irrevocable and definitive moment of coincidence in the personal history of Jesus.[45]

To recognise this is to begin to understand what it means to say, and how we can claim, that Jesus is known to be true God by being true man. Humanity mediates divinity when as in the case of Jesus it not only reaches but also realises the final goal of its transcendent drive which is God himself. It is within this double horizon of the biblical and theological understanding of man that the Chalcedonian dogma of Jesus as true God and true man can begin to assume universal significance for us today.

9 Relocating the dogma of the Incarnation

In our last chapter we saw how it was possible to free the divinity of Jesus from the technical terms of substance, nature and person by resituating it within the broader context of God and man. This gave rise to an exposition of Jesus as true God and true man followed by an anthropological explanation of how in fact humanity can mediate divinity. We must now continue these reflections and apply their implications to the dogma of the Incarnation. This will involve in the spirit of our last chapter, a widening of christological horizons so that the Incarnation can appear, where it properly belongs, as the interlocking link between God and man. Once this happens it will become clear that it is only in and through the mystery of Jesus Christ as the Word incarnate that we can truly begin to probe the absolute mystery of God in himself.

Creation and Incarnation

When one understands the divinity of Jesus in terms of perfective humanity mediating divinity, and explains this perfection of humanity as the unique point of contact between God's self-communication to man and man's self-transcendent drive towards God, then one is in fact already reflecting upon the dogma of the Incarnation. The Incarnation is the coming together of God and man in Jesus. This coming together takes place through the grace of the self-descending communication of God reaching out and touching the self-ascending transcendent being of man in Jesus.[1] Thus the dogma of the Incarnation represents the peak point of God-man and man-God contact. The divine-human and the human-divine threshold of life has been crossed in the mystery of Jesus Christ as the Word Incarnate. We have already seen how this is possible in our analysis of God as a reality who gracefully suffuses himself throughout the world and of man as a being who has an infinite capacity for self-transcendence.

Another way of expressing this profound mystery of "God made man" is to say that the fullest and most organic integration of Godhead and manhood as we have described these terms has taken place in Jesus of Nazareth. The furthest reach of God into the life of man and the richest response of man in loving surrender has been realised in Jesus to such an extent that we can say in all truth that he is "God made man".[2] Alternatively, one could describe the Incarnation as "the conjunction of God's giving and man's receiving in Jesus Christ"[3] or again, as the paradoxical meeting point of God's grace and man's freedom.[4] Whichever set of categories one decides to adopt, be it those of God's self-communication and man's self-transcendence, or God reaching into life and man responding, or divine giving and human receiving, or the paradox of grace and freedom, this divine mystery must be seen as something anchored in the radical nature of God and of man.

On the other hand once we begin to see the mystery of the Incarnation within these categories as the unique point of contact between God and man within history then it becomes necessary to explain the extent to which God and man meet in Jesus. It was in an attempt to define precisely this relationship between Jesus and God that the doctrine of the hypostatic union was defined by the councils of Ephesus and Chalcedon. The mystery of the Incarnation is not just an extension of the creature-creator relationship, nor is it merely the coming together of God and man in

Jesus, nor is it simply the instance of another divine—
human dialogue. It is all of these and much more
besides. The mystery of the Incarnation is the real hypostatic union of God and man and man and God in Jesus of
Nazareth. This union of God and man in Jesus is an absolute and complete union so that we can say that Jesus is the
Word Incarnate and mean by this that Jesus is the divine
person (*hypostasis*) of the *Logos,* who is the perfect self-
expression of God, made flesh. This is possible because only
God without ceasing to be God, can constitute a being in
distinction from himself which in virtue of its origin is radically dependent and autonomous at one and the same time.
This radical dependency and autonomy which exists in
Jesus as the person of the divine *Logos* made flesh is based
on the paradox in life that grace and freedom grow in
direct, not inverse, proportion to each other.[5]

In other words the coming together of God and man
in Jesus is a more intense, different, and new coming
together in contrast to the overall God-man relationship
in the world and yet it remains within that general framework. However, this element of newness within the mystery
of the Incarnation must not be so emphasised or exaggerated that it becomes unrecognisable or meaningless. A
balance between sameness and difference, between continuity and discontinuity, in regard to the relationship between
God and man in others and in Jesus is called for here.
Jesus is different in kind in his relationship with God but
not to the extent that he becomes isolated from the rest
of mankind with whom he has fully identified. This difference in kind is based on his difference in degree from the
rest of mankind.[6]

Ultimately of course the dogma of the Incarnation
goes back to the life, death and resurrection of Jesus.
The experience by the apostles of this historical datum
was such that they could say upon reflection that they
had encountered God in human form. This faith insight
into the mystery of the man Jesus gave rise to a variety

of formulations concerning his divinity. As the divinity of Jesus became clear the dogma of the Incarnation gradually unfolded itself upon the consciousness of the infant Church. In reality of course the divinity of Jesus and the dogma of the Incarnation are one and the same single mystery. However within the perspective of a low-ascending christology the divinity of Jesus would seem to have a logical priority over the Incarnation in the order of knowing and understanding. In a certain sense the dogma of the Incarnation is a commentary upon the implications and significance of the divinity of Jesus. This does not mean the doctrine of the Incarnation is a subsequent addition to the mystery of Jesus Christ. Rather the reality of the Incarnation is a mystery that was present throughout the life of Jesus which like the divinity was only progressively disclosed to the apostles in their experience and reflection upon his life, death and resurrection.

The traditional formulation of the dogma of the Incarnation states that "God became man in Jesus of Nazareth". As such this statement means what it says namely that God identified fully with humanity in the man Jesus, or as St John states so tersely "the Word was made flesh and dwelt among us" (*Jn 1:14*). It does not mean that God came down on earth and walked around disguised in the fancy dress of humanity pretending to be a man. It was precisely this kind of pretence that the Church firmly rejected in her protest against Gnosticism and Docetism. Nor does it mean that God simply became God in Jesus. This too has been ruled out by the Church in her opposition to Apollinarianism, Monophysitism, and Monothelitism. Instead the Incarnation means that God entered fully and unconditionally into human life in the man Jesus. God enfleshed, en-manned, and othered himself totally in Jesus so that in experiencing the man Jesus the apostles also experienced God as personally present in their midst. Anything short of this borders on the frontiers of superstition and mythology.

One of the great difficulties in the past with our understanding of the Incarnation, which we have already alluded to, is that it tended to become divorced from our understanding of God's gracious presence throughout creation. As a result the Incarnation appeared as a "bolt out of the blue" giving one the impression that it was some kind of "anomalous exception" to the ordinary everyday presence of God in the world.[7] In recent times, however, Catholic theology has returned to an older and more integrated vision of the Incarnation which sees it as the high point of a continuous drama in which the natural and the supernatural interpenetrate each other. Within this vision there is an underlying unity between creation and Incarnation.[8] Creation, or better, the underlying presence of God in the world is that reality which is ordained towards the mystery of the Incarnation.[9] The goal of creation is Incarnation so that in a real sense creation only reaches its point of completion in and through the reality of Incarnation.[10]

This vision goes back to the Pauline theology of the cosmic Christ. There Jesus Christ is presented as "the first born of all creation" (*Col 1:15*); he is "the head" (*Eph 1:22*) who "unites all things in heaven and all things on earth" (*Eph 1:10*). This picture of the cosmic Christ is taken up by Irenaeus of Lyons who visualises man and creation as realities growing towards a point of perfection which find their fulfilment in Jesus Christ.[11] For Irenaeus the mystery of Jesus Christ is the point of recapitulation which not only recovers what was there from the beginning in its infancy but also now brings it to completion. This vision was taken up later by Duns Scotus (d. 1308) and his school who gave it an explicitly incarnational twist. They pointed out that the Incarnation would have taken place irrespective of the reality of sin. They saw the Incarnation as something intrinsic to the first and primary intention within the divine plan of creation and not simply as a subsequent secondary intention in the light of sin. At the same time, however, the Scotists did acknowledge that for us in our given sinful situation the Incarnation took on an explicitly redemptive character whereby man was freed from sin and restored to fellowship with God. This Scotist position differed from that of the Thomistic school which saw the primary purpose of the Incarnation as the salvation of man from sin with the implication that had man not sinned the Incarnation would not have occurred. Today in the twentieth century the Scotist position has come to the fore under the influence of the evolutionary outlook and its theological application to the person of Jesus Christ.[12] It is this revitalised vision, more than anything else, that has contributed to a renewal of our understanding of the Incarnation and its relocation as the climax of creation. Within this understanding the Incarnation appears as the explicitation of God's gracious presence in creation. As such the Incarnation is the supreme exemplification in a uniquely human way of a divine pattern which is already given in creation itself. The Incarnation therefore is not an isolated exception but rather the definitive culmination of a process already set in motion through the gift of creation. To this extent creation is the basis of Incarnation and Incarnation is the fullness of creation. In a certain sense creation is itself a form of "incarnation"[13] in that it mediates however obscurely traces of the divine power and presence which become formalised in the Christ-Event. It is against this background of creation as "incarnational" in the broad sense that we must see the mystery of Jesus Christ as the Incarnation of God.

Within this presentation of the dogma of the Incarnation it is important to stress once again that we are dealing with the mystery of God as a reality present in creation through the outgoing activity of his self-communication to man in the world. This conception of God exists in direct contrast to the view which simply sees God as a being locked up in his own lofty transcendence who occasionally

intervenes in order to reveal himself. This latter outlook on
God is no longer acceptable philosophically or theologically in the light of modern science. Instead we must begin
with an understanding of God which accepts that he is
personally involved with our world from creation onwards.
If our understanding of God in Jesus becomes divorced
from our perception of God in creation then it is no
longer the God of Abraham, of Isaac, and of Jacob that
we are dealing with but rather some Platonic construct
or idol of the imagination which we are trying to manipulate and incarnate in Jesus of Nazareth.

When we relocate the mystery of the Incarnation
therefore within the context of God's presence throughout
creation it becomes clear that the mystery of the Word
Incarnate is not some unnatural or atypical divine
gesture. On the contrary the incarnation of God in Jesus
is the unambiguous and definitive revelation of a divine
presence which is all around us. The Incarnation therefore is not the manifestation of a presence which was pre-
viously absent but rather the special incidence of a divine
omnipresence in the world at large. Within this unique
instance God is at his most typical in that the universal
self-communication of God throughout the world becomes
particularised and personified in Jesus Christ. As such
this particularisation and personification of God's self-
communication in Jesus is perfectly consistent and quite
in character with his overall self-communication in creation.[14]

Finally, within this more unified scheme of things
the Incarnation no longer appears as some kind of after-
thought by a fickle-minded God who suddenly decided
to introduce himself into a world which he perfectly
created and which later went astray through sin and
which he therefore decided to abandon. On the contrary,
creation from the beginning is orientated towards Incarnation.[15] The whole movement of creation is directed
towards the final inbreaking of the divine into the human

and the human into the divine which has now taken
place in the Incarnation. Creation, which has always
been graced by the divine presence, is "the prior setting
and condition" for God's absolute self-communication to
man.[16] In both instances the initiative rests with God's
gracious gift of himself.

Incarnation and the mystery of God

Having relocated the Incarnation within the mainstream
of God's universal presence in creation we must now say
something about the significance of the Word Incarnate
for our understanding of the mystery of God. Here it
must be pointed out that the reality of the Incarnation
first and foremost lights up our experience of God's mysterious presence in the world around us and in doing so
brings us into a new consciousness of the divine mystery.
The Incarnation does this by providing us with a new
way of looking at the world we live in. It implies that
the gulf between heaven and earth, between God and
man, between the supernatural and the natural, between
the sacred and the secular, which incidentally was never
absolute but always threatening to become so due to sin,
has once and for all been overcome so that now we can
glimpse heaven on earth, God in man, the supernatural
in the natural, and the sacred amidst the secular. There
can be no doubt that the God of the Old Testament
tended to appear, no matter how incorrectly, as one who
was removed from us existing up there in heaven looking
down upon earth, whereas the God whom we now confess
in Jesus Christ is right here where we are and can only
be found here in the world.[17] As a result of the Christ-
Event therefore we can say that God is no longer a
stranger or an outsider to our world but one who is to be
found with us, Immanuel, at the centre of life which is
throbbing with his Incarnate presence. In the light of the
Incarnation it must also be said that there is nothing here
on earth which is exclusively profane for those who have

the eyes to see.[18] The whole of created reality, especially
living humanity and in particular the humanity of Jesus
as found in the body of his community, the Church,
reflects, mediates, and Incarnates the power and presence
of God in our world in different ways.

On the level of created reality it is important to
remember that in virtue of the Incarnation the finite has
been given an infinite depth and can no longer be simply
regarded as something opposite or opposed to the infinite.
The whole of created reality has received an infinite extension by the fact that it has become in Jesus Christ as
its cosmic centre the vehicle of God's Incarnate presence.
All things hold together in Jesus as the Incarnate Word
in whom they exist (*Col 1:17*), and therefore all things
possess an unfathomable depth which Christian faith
alone can sound.[19]

On the level of living humanity it must be pointed
out that it is here perhaps more than anywhere else that
the greatest challenge issuing from the mystery of the
Incarnation emerges. This has been brought out by the
Second Vatican Council which in its *Pastoral Constitution
on the Church in the Modern World* states:

> The truth is that *only in the mystery of the Incarnate
> Word does the mystery of man take on light* . . . .
> Christ the final Adam, by the revelation of the
> mystery of the Father . . . fully *reveals man to man
> and makes his supreme calling clear*.[20]

We have already seen something of the *mystery of
man* coming into full view through the mystery of Jesus
Christ in which the perfection of humanity mediates
divinity so that by being true Man Jesus is true God.
The *revelation of man to man* takes place through Jesus
who realises in the fullest possible way the graced capacities of man and thereby incarnates a real (hypostatic)

unity between God and man. Because Jesus embodies this unity between God and man he also manifests at the same time the *supreme calling* of man. This supreme calling which issues from the Incarnation challenges man on a two-fold basis.

On the one hand the Incarnation invites man to "put on Christ" in the fundamental sense of incarnating in his own personal life the real God-man and man-God unity that was realised in Jesus. In this regard it is important to remember that the achievement of Incarnation by Jesus was not simply an instantaneous happening but rather a progressive realisation of God's unique self-communication addressed to the self-transcendent openness of Jesus which was there from the beginning.[21] To be sure, the mystery of the Incarnation was instituted in Jesus from the moment of his conception onwards, but the working out of this unique event took place historically through the life, death and resurrection of Jesus. In particular it was cemented through different moments such as doing good, combating evil, overcoming temptation, leading a life of prayer, and maintaining a radically theocentric outlook, each of which in its own way contributed to the crystallisation of the God-man and man-God unity in Jesus. In the same way every individual is invited to respond to the different modes of God's gracious self-communicating presence in the world, which are constantly summoning him so that he may grow in his own God-man and man-God unity under the inspiration of Jesus Christ as the Word Incarnate.

On the other hand man is also called upon to recognise the presence of this same divine mystery taking place in others around him. When we encounter the "other" we are not simply encountering "an-other" but rather someone who is here and now for us the medium of God's Incarnate grace in the world. It is here that Christian doctrine and morality mutually complement each other in that the mystery of the Incarnation with its challenge

for man clarifies the import of the great moral commandment of love of God through love of neighbour.[22]

Thirdly, on the level of the Christian community
which is the enduring body of Christ in the world constituting the Church we have the permanent presence of
the Incarnate Word in our midst.[23] As the Second Vatican
Council pointed out, the reality of the Church "may be
compared to the mystery of the Incarnate Word"[24] in that
the Church is similarly composed of human and divine
elements. Like the mystery which it represents the Church
mediates the divine in and through the human so that
the more human the Church is in the spirit of its founder
Jesus Christ, the more obvious will its divine origin
become. It is in this sense that the Church is the continuation or extension of the Incarnation and is thereby the
universal sacrament of God's salvation in the world.[25] As
the universal sacrament of God's salvation she incarnates
through her individual sacraments and in particular
through the Eucharist the universal saving presence of
God's self-communication which is taking place all around
us in ordinary everyday life. To this extent all ecclesiology
and by extension sacramental theology is inspired by the
incarnational principle as founded upon and derived from
the mystery of the Incarnation.

In the light of these three levels of Incarnational presence of the Word in the world it should be clear that the
Incarnation is no mere transient episode of God's activity
in the world which momentarily erupted two thousand
years ago and then subsequently disappeared. Instead the
mystery of the Incarnation is an on-going reality which
is continually taking place in different degrees all around
us if we have the eyes of Christian faith to recognise it.
The truth of this claim is already implied in the great
commandment of love of God through love of man and
the universal identification of Jesus with "the least of
these my brethren" (Mt 25:40; 45). Further, the mystery
of the Incarnation as the climactic completion of creation

has, as we have just seen above, an irrevocable influence upon everything subsequent to it. An incarnational process has been inaugurated by Jesus Christ which will only reach full completion in and through the second coming of the Word Incarnate[26] when the world will become totally transparent to its divine centre in Jesus Christ. In the meantime this process of Incarnation centred in Jesus Christ is taking place around us as "the final term of a creation which is still continuing everywhere".[27]

Of course it must be acknowledged that this ongoing presence of Incarnation in our world is never as clear or as complete as it was in Jesus of Nazareth. The reality of the Incarnation around us is fragile, always allowing of more or less, due to the persistent presence of sinfulness and selfishness. Yet the grace and offer of Incarnation both in our own lives and in the lives of others is always there as a challenge beckoning us to become Christ-like by being receptive to God's omnipresent self-communication.

This suggestion that the Incarnation is a mystery continually taking place around us in the light of the mystery of Jesus Christ is acknowledged by the Second Vatican Council when it points out that "by his Incarnation the Son of God has united himself in some fashion with every man".[28] Here the Council clearly recognises the equality, the dignity, and the sacredness of each and every individual as the vehicle of God's incarnate grace. As a result the centre of our encounter with God is our brother and sister with whom God has united himself. There can be no going back therefore on what has happened to the heart of humanity in Jesus Christ. The mystery of the Incarnation as past event and present challenge is there inviting us to dig deep into the heart of man and his universe to discover that they are shimmering with divinity.[29] Most of all the mystery of the Incarnation as the meeting point between God and man is the supreme paradigm for all human encounter with God.

The theocentric character of christology

The real value of placing the Incarnation within the context of creation and seeing it as the climactic point which lights up our experience of God in the world is that it reintroduces the mystery of Jesus Christ into the mystery of God. For too long christology has been divorced from theology (*Logos/Theos*). Indeed at times christology tended to become an end in itself. This can be seen in certain forms of myopic christocentricism which can be misleading. Christocentricism is necessary as a means towards an end, but once it becomes an end in itself then the universal significance of the Christ-Event is obscured and the mystery of God forgotten. To concentrate on the Christ-Event to the exclusion of its bearing on God as some have done in the past is to run the risk of reductionism. It was precisely this kind of phenomenon which took place in the middle sixties giving rise to Jesusology, the death of God theology, and atheistic Christianity.[30]

In opposition to such tendencies it must be affirmed that the ultimate purpose of christology is to illuminate our experience and understanding of the mystery of God. Christology if it is to achieve this goal must be theocentric. One of the basic themes running through our essay on christology is that one must begin from a background that acknowledges in some elementary way, no matter how primitively or privately, the presence of an underlying mystery in life which we call God. It is from this intuitive grasp of a deeper dimension to life that we turn to Jesus so as to enlarge our awareness and understanding of this abiding mystery in life. In fact strictly speaking it is this underlying reality of God which constitutes the one absolute mystery and which therefore defines all other mysteries including the mystery of Jesus Christ.[31] The final task of christology therefore is to bring us nearer to this absolute inexpressible mystery we call God, without claiming to exhaust this fundamental mystery. It does this particularly through the doctrine of the Incarnation which, as we have seen, understands the man Jesus as the concrete embodiment of God in the world who opens up for us the deeper dimensions of life. There exists or should exist an underlying relationship between the mystery of Jesus Christ and the mystery of God: this relationship should be one of creative tension whereby the mystery of Jesus Christ, once it is grasped in faith, throws us back dialectically upon the absolute mystery of God with a new and enlightened consciousness. Thus there exists a certain to-ing and fro-ing between the mystery of Jesus Christ and the mystery of God. It is in this sense that all christology is theocentric.

In particular terms this means that the mystery of Jesus Christ opens up for us the inexhaustible riches of the mystery of God. We must never simply stop with the mystery of Jesus Christ. Instead we must move from Jesus Christ into the mystery of God. Because God has shown his face to us in the man Jesus which is what the dogma of the Incarnation implies we now have a new mode of access to the inexhaustible mystery of God. Thus Jesus is the clue or better the meaning (*logos*) to the ultimate mystery of life itself.[32] As such Jesus brings into "focus" for us the mystery of God which is present and active throughout life.[33] In this way the person of Jesus Christ provides us with a new posture of consciousness *vis-à-vis* the basic mystery of God at work in the world.

This theocentric character of christology is clearly brought out by the great theologians of the New Testament. St Paul frequently talks about the mystery (*mysterion*) hidden for ages in God which is now made known to us through Jesus Christ (*Ep 1:9; 3:9*), so that Jesus appears as "the secret plan of God" (*Col 1:27; 2:2*). Yet this mystery of God which has been manifested in Jesus Christ will only be fully revealed at the end of time. This manifestation of the mystery which has taken place in Jesus in no way removes the richness of the mystery in itself. Instead Jesus by opening up the mystery of God compels us to dig deeper into the heart of reality.

A similar type of theocentric stress is to be found in St John. This is best exemplified in the "Farewell Discourse" and the Philip incident:

> "Let not your hearts be troubled; believe in God, believe also in me. . . . And when I go and prepare a place for you, I will come again. . . . And you know the way where I am going."

> Thomas said to him: "Lord, we do not know where you are going; how can we know the way?"

> Jesus said to him: "I am the Way, and the Truth, and the Life; no one comes to the Father, but by me. If you had known me, you would have known my Father also; henceforth you know him and have seen him."

> Philip said to him: "Lord, show us the Father, and we shall be satisfied."

> Jesus said to him: "Have I been with you so long, and yet you do not know me, Philip? He who has seen me has seen the Father; how can you say, 'Show us the Father'? Do you not believe that I am in the Father and the Father in me?" (*Jn 14:1-10*)

The historical background to these verses is not important here. Much more to the point is the theocentric character of christology which they suggest. The context of this discourse is the departure of Jesus and the despondency of his disciples. Jesus tries to reassure his disciples by appealing to them to believe in God (whose Kingdom he has been heralding) and to believe in himself. The apostles, however, fail to see the connection in this double appeal for belief. Jesus is forced to spell out his role in this belief in God by stating explicitly that he is "the Way, the Truth and the Life; no one comes to the Father but by me" (*Jn 14:6*). Whatever interpretation one gives to these words the overall import is clear. One can only come to full belief in and understanding of the mystery of God in and through Jesus. In fact Jesus is presenting himself as the way which leads to the ultimate mystery of God, as the truth opening up the absolute truth of God, and as the life introducing us to the eternal life of God, or, as some prefer to hold, Jesus is the Way because he is *the* truth and *the* life.[34] The goal of this Way is the reality of God himself. Yet Philip fails to appreciate the significance of what Jesus is saying and blurts out rather impatiently "but show us God the Father and then all will be clear". Of course there is a touch of the Philip in us all: "If only we could see God just once it would be so much easier." Gently but firmly Jesus explains to Philip that "he who has seen me has seen the Father". By this Jesus is not claiming, as is sometimes thought, that there is an absolute unqualified identity between himself and God the Father. Rather Jesus is suggesting that by seeing him we see the way *to* God the Father; he is pointing beyond himself to that reality whose power and presence he has been proclaiming throughout his life. It is this reality of God, around which the whole mission of Jesus is centred, that is now brought nearer to us in and through the mystery of Jesus Christ. In fact to be a Christian is to be one who approaches the absolute mystery of God in and through the Person of Jesus Christ. Finally this theocentric character of christology is further evidenced and highlighted by the permanent tradition within Christianity that all prayer and worship takes place through Jesus Christ our Lord. Consequently we address God as Father through Jesus Christ in the Spirit. It is this type of theocentric christology that makes up the basic structure of the entire liturgy which is theocentric by being christocentric.

Ultimately of course the validity of this christocentric theocentricism stands or falls on the seriousness with which we take the mystery of the Incarnation. If we accept, as the doctrine of the Incarnation challenges us to accept, that God has personally communicated himself to us in the man Jesus, then we must acknowledge the logic of this involvement of God in our world which is that we now approach God in and through the reality of this concrete mediation which is the mystery of Jesus Christ. Without this acceptance of the Incarnation Christianity is both incoherent and inadequate. With this acceptance of the Incarnation Christianity shows up the incoherence and inadequacy of non-incarnational theism.[35]

10 A return to the historical roots of christology in Jesus

In this our last chapter we must return to our original starting point, namely that of the historical Jesus. This will afford an opportunity of drawing together some of the loose ends which we left behind us in the course of our essay. Such loose ends include the significance of the historical minimum concerning the life of Jesus which biblical research yielded and the question about the relationship that exists between this historical minimum and christology. Both of these issues centre around the question of the unity or lack of unity that exists between the Jesus of history and the Christ of faith. This question was raised in chapter two and then peacefully laid to rest. It must now be re-opened. One of the difficulties about most discussions on the Jesus of history and Christ of faith issue is that too often they assume the discovery and the content of the Christ of faith. For this reason it seems more appropriate to discuss this question at the end after we have established the existence and the content of the Christ of faith in the life of the Church.

The permanent significance of the historical Jesus for christology

It should be clear in the light of our gradual ascent from a "low" to a "high" christology that the basic irreducible point of departure for any consideration of the foundations of Christianity is the life of the historical Jesus. One of the most distinctive features about Christianity is the fact that

147

it is rooted and grounded in the life of a historical person. This fact is particularly important today when Christianity is beginning to encounter ecumenically the other great religions of the world. For instance, it is a matter of surprise, for the Hindu, to discover that the claims of Christianity are centred around real historical events.[1] To ignore this historical character of Christianity would be to relegate it to the unimportant status of being just another contingent religion without a founder.[2] Instead the historicity of Christianity must be asserted and with it the "scandal of particularity" which is thereby implied.

The truth of these general observations becomes quite clear when one confronts the christological claims of the Christian religion. Within such a confrontation there are two central areas which highlight the importance of the historical Jesus. These are a balanced understanding of the kerygma of the Church and the whole question of the origins of Christian faith.

If the kerygma of the Church, the proclamation that Jesus Christ is Lord, is to be protected from becoming some kind of Gnostic or Docetic construct then it must constantly be controlled by reference to the historical life of Jesus. For some strange reason there has been a tendency to associate christological Gnosticism and Docetism exclusively with the growth of Christianity into the Hellenistic world during the first few centuries of its missionary expansion. In reality, however, the possibility of christological Gnosticism and Docetism is as much a threat today as it was in the past.

Shades of such Gnosticism can be found today in the adherence by some to certain forms of mystery religions from the East. Similar shades of Gnosticism also exist amongst those groups which require subscription to a catalogue of so-called orthodox Christian doctrine as the primary means to "saving one's soul".[3] As for Docetism, the view that Jesus was not really a man like unto us in all things sin excepted, with all that this implies, is still not uncommon today. The only way of countering these erroneous views is by returning to a critical study of the life of the historical Jesus. Although the details of such a study may vary it is nonetheless possible, as we have seen, to map out a hard historical nucleus of reliable data about the life of Jesus. We have already seen the type of picture which emerges concerning the historical Jesus. It is only within and against this historical picture of Jesus that the kerygma of the Church can be preserved from Gnostic and Docetic tendencies.

In reality the only means we have at our disposal for preventing the creation of mythical ideas about Jesus Christ is the return to a historical study of the life of Jesus. To this extent historical research into the gospels must be seen as a permanent and necessary feature of contemporary christology which safeguards our understanding of the full mystery of Jesus Christ. Once the kerygma or what is commonly called the Christ of faith becomes divorced from the historical Jesus then there is always a danger that it will evaporate into "mere noise and smoke".[4] When this type of contact with the historical Jesus is severed it means in effect that the historical particularity and personal humanity of Jesus is lost, both of which are essential to a proper understanding of the Christ-Event and its universal significance. Every return to the historical Jesus is of course at the same time a return to the humanity of Jesus which as we have already seen is essential for understanding the divinity of Jesus. Consequently by going back to the historical Jesus we are also eliminating what Rahner calls the persistent presence of Monophysitism in our thinking about Jesus Christ.[5] As a general rule we can say that the "higher" christology tends to become, the greater the need to return to the historical Jesus as a source and check.

These remarks have a most practical bearing on our preaching and teaching of the mystery of Jesus Christ. There will always be a temptation in presenting Jesus Christ to romanticise about the life of Jesus in a way that has

no basis in history. This gives rise to a type of historical
fiction about Jesus who was everything, especially in the
realm of superlatives, which is somewhat reminiscent of the
"liberal lives" of the nineteenth century. When this happens
it is only a matter of time before christological judgments
which have no historical warrant are created. In each
instance not only is the integrity of preaching and teaching
called into question[6] but a serious state of historical scepticism sets in which refuses to accept the most obvious
things about the life of Jesus. Once again the only check
and control against this kind of abuse is a return to a
critical outline of the life of Jesus which is based on historical research and which openly acknowledges the limitations of our knowledge about that life.

The other central area of christology in which the
historical Jesus plays an important role is that of the
formation of Christian faith. Our analysis of the Christ-
Event revealed that it was the life of the historical Jesus
which provided the basic material for confessing Jesus as
the Christ who is the Lord. The coming to be of full-
blown Christian faith took place against the background
of the historical life of Jesus. In fact some knowledge and
understanding of the historical life of Jesus is essential
to the formation of Christian faith. This is certainly the
case with the apostles and would also seem to be the case
for those who come after the apostles.

In the case of the apostles the different words and
deeds of the historical Jesus evoked a personal faith response. Instances of this faith response can be seen in the
type of stance assumed by the apostles towards Jesus in
his earthly ministry. Historical realities like the proclamation of the Kingdom of God, the promise of salvation, the
performance of exorcism, the working of miracles, the
claim to authority, the forgiving of sins, the setting up of
a new table fellowship, the existence of a filial relation towards God as Father, and the overriding presence of an
eschatological ethos in the life of Jesus demanded a definite

response from the apostles. The type of response evoked
from the apostles during the pre-paschal stage would have
been one of basic religious faith which was informed by
the Jewish traditions, which were now being renewed in
Jesus of Nazareth. It could be described as basic-Jewish-
faith which had now become centred around Jesus in the
hope that he would be the one who would redeem Israel
(*Lk 24:21*). As such it was this basic-Jewish-faith in hope
centred around Jesus which was transformed into Christian faith through the Resurrection experience. The paschal
experience added a new dimension to the apostolic faith-
understanding of Jesus whom they now recognise as Christ
and Lord who embodies the eschatological grace of God's
reign on earth. This new dimension must not be understood adoptionistically as if the person of Jesus was
changed substantially by the paschal event. Rather the
personal object of faith is now understood more explicitly
and comprehensively in the light of the Easter Event. The
Resurrection-Pentecostal experience draws out the full
implication of what was taking place in the historical life
of Jesus.

To simplify, one could say that the formation of
Christian faith in the lives of the apostles took place in
different stages. Early on there was a kind of inchoate or
implicit faith demanded by the historical Jesus in his
public ministry. This then is followed by the formation of
full and explicit christological faith in the light of the
paschal experience.[7] The life of the historical Jesus dis-
posed and prepared the apostles for the inbreaking of
God's reign which took place through the Resurrection.
It would have been impossible for the apostles to appreciate the eschatological significance of the Resurrection
without this prior preaching and teaching.

Significantly it is this type of sequence in the formation of Christian faith which is implied in recent documents from the Catholic Church. The 1964 Instruction
which we have already referred to talks about "the fuller

understanding"[8] which the apostles have of Jesus after the Resurrection experience. The Decree on *Divine Revelation* which incorporates this part of the 1964 Instruction points out that Jesus perfected revelation through his "words and deeds, his signs and wonders *but especially* through his death and glorious resurrection from the dead and final sending of the Spirit".[9] This clearly suggests that a progressive development took place in the formation of the apostles' faith understanding, a development which began with the historical words and deeds of Jesus and achieved full maturity in the recognition of Jesus as the risen Christ and reigning Lord.

A somewhat similar process would seem to take place in the life of the individual Christian when he comes to personally appropriate the gift of faith in Jesus Christ which he has received from the Christian community. The background against which this assimilation of Christian faith takes place is that of the individual's basic faith experiences of God's gracious presence in the world. From this background he will accept the gift of Christian faith which is offered from the community as a concretisation, clarification, and definition of his own basic faith experiences. In doing so he will be driven, sooner or later, to search out the ultimate origin and source of this Christian faith. This search will take him back to the life of the historical Jesus as the base and historical foundation of Christian faith. After returning to the life of Jesus he will then move forward in the footsteps of the apostles to discover Jesus as the Christ who is Lord in the light of the resurrection. In addition he will also discover that it is this mystery of the resurrection which is the basis of his present invitation to Christian faith in that it is as a result of the resurrection that Jesus can live on in his community offering himself as gift to man. The fact that some who enjoy the tranquillity of Christian faith from beginning to end never make this return to the origins is no argument against the validity of such a movement for those who, for whatever reason, be it a crisis, a search, a purifying development, or even a de-institutionalisation of Christian faith, are driven in the direction of this movement.

The emerging point here is that the historical Jesus stands out as an integral part of full-blown Christian faith. This is not to suggest that the historical Jesus is the new object of Christian faith as some of the Post-Bultmannians seem to imply.[10] Rather the historical Jesus is the foundation stone for the development of Christian faith. The historical Jesus as known to us through Biblical research in all his different words and deeds is therefore constitutive for the formation of Christian faith. It is not enough to suggest as Bultmann does that it is merely the existence of Jesus in his givenness without historical details that lies behind Christian faith. To affirm such a Christ of faith without historical details would be to accept a content-less, characterless, and impersonal reality as the object of faith. Rather if as the early Post-Bultmannians pointed out the person to whom the Christ of faith refers is in no way concretely definable in his historicity then he becomes pure myth.[11]

In the end the legitimation of our confession of Jesus as Lord must go back to the historical Jesus and once legitimated this Christian faith must remain in close contact with the historical Jesus if it is to remain integral. Otherwise the kerygma without Jesus becomes a verbal vacuum and Jesus without the kerygma appears as a meaningless surd.[12] It is in this sense that the historical Jesus assumes a position of permanent significance within christology which no one can afford to neglect.

The relationship between the Jesus of history and the Christ of faith

Within this position of permanent significance that obtains between the historical Jesus and christology the question arises as to what kind of relationship exists between the Jesus of history and the Christ of faith. We saw earlier in our examination of the Christ-Event that the words and deeds of the historical Jesus gave rise to his death and that his death was the horizon against which the mystery of the resurrection unfolded itself. It was within this unified development that the gradual transition from the Jesus of history to the Christ of faith took place. Within this gradual transition there is first and foremost a fundamental relationship of underlying continuity between the Jesus of history and the Christ of faith. This relationship is one of personal continuity. The person referred to in the concrete historical life of Jesus is exactly the same as the person contained in the living reality of the risen Christ of faith. To ignore or to deny this line of personal continuity would be tantamount to suggesting that the Jesus of history and the Christ of faith are two different and distinct realities whereas the whole thrust of our exposition of the Christ-Event has been to vindicate that they are one and the same personal reality. It is true that the impact of biblical research in the nineteenth century drove a wedge between the Jesus of history and the Christ of faith. However we have indicated earlier in this study how this temporary barrier between Jesus and Christ can be removed by applying the advances of biblical research to the gospel account of Jesus Christ. As a result it is now possible to say under the full glare of historical criticism that the Jesus of history is the Christ of faith and that the Christ of faith is a flowering forth of the implications of the life, death and resurrection of Jesus. Furthermore we saw in our analysis of the evidence for the resurrection that the evangelists go to great trouble to drive home the continuity between the crucified Jesus of history and the risen Christ of faith. They do this through their colourful descriptions of "eating", "touching" and "talking" with the risen Jesus. As already noted the purpose behind these

rather physical descriptions of the resurrection is to indicate the oneness and sameness between the Jesus whom
they had known according to the flesh and the Jesus
whom they now encounter after death. Another index of
this emphasis on continuity can be found in the empty
tomb story. The actual emptiness of the tomb would seem
to suggest some form of personal continuity between the
Jesus of history and the Christ of faith.[13]

The reality of this continuity between the Jesus of
history and the Christ of faith may be illustrated in different ways. This can be done by looking over our gradual
ascent from Jesus as a man among men to Jesus as the
Christ who is the Lord. In doing so it is possible to detect
at least three distinct levels of continuity between the
Jesus of history and the Christ of faith.

On the one hand we saw how the words and deeds
of Jesus gave rise to his death and resurrection and how
the death and resurrection explain the meaning of his
words and deeds. Separated from his earthly ministry the
death of Jesus becomes a disaster and the resurrection
appears as a mere prodigy. The resurrection must never
be seen as something which imposes a meaning on the
life of Jesus from the outside as if it were some *coup de
force*. Rather the resurrection clarifies what is already imminent in the words and deeds of Jesus.[14] The eschatological suggestiveness of the words and deeds of Jesus such
as the announcement of the Kingdom of God, the critical
call to repentance, the setting up of a new table fellowship, and the promise of salvation is the background
against which the resurrection experience unfolds itself
meaningfully upon the consciousness of the apostles in
terms of the dawning of a new era. Traces of this kind of
understanding can be seen in the response of the Palestinian community to the Easter-Event. It is by this progressive unfolding of eschatological meaning through the
experience of the life, death and resurrection of Jesus as a
unified whole that the first level of continuity between the

Jesus of history and the Christ of faith becomes clear. This level of continuity may be classified as one of eschatological continuity that exists between the Jesus of history and the Christ of faith.

Another form of continuity between the Jesus of history and the Christ of faith can be discerned on the level of implicit and explicit christology respectively. Evidence for the presence of an implicit christology in the life of Jesus can be found in the prefacing of his sayings with the expression "Amen",[15] the addressing of God as Father, the existence of a filial relationship towards God, the teaching contained in his parables, and the forgiving of sins. It was on the basis of these historical phenomena in the life of Jesus that the apostles could attribute in the light of the resurrection different biblical titles to Jesus, such as "the Christ", "Lord", "Son of God", and "the Word" which in fact make up the content of explicit christology. Not only that, but because of this continuity between the Jesus of history and the Christ of faith the Evangelists have no scruple in projecting back the post-paschal titles into the earthly life of Jesus. Thus on the level of christology we can say that there is also a basic continuity between the Jesus of history and the Christ of faith.

Thirdly there is a continuity between the Jesus of history and the Christ of faith on the level of faith itself.[16] By this we mean that the faith of the Jesus of history as the founder of Christianity is continued in the Christian faith of his followers. To fully appreciate this point we must first of all situate the faith of Jesus as a reality which is continuous with the basic faith of Judaism. This point of insertion between the faith of Jesus and the basic faith of Judaism occurs in the acceptance by Jesus, as evidenced in his preaching, that the power and presence of God is a reality imminent in his own life. Jesus believed in faith that the Kingdom of God was being made manifest through his missionary activity. It is this faith of

Jesus which inspires the faith (in hope) of the apostles in his own person. As such this faith of Jesus is continued after the resurrection in Christian faith which now recognises Jesus as *the* one in whom the power and presence of God has been fully realised and through whom the Kingdom of God is made manifest as present reality and future promise. In particular the faith of Jesus is enshrined in Christian faith which now accepts God as gracefully present in the most ordinary and human experiences of life such as universal love of neighbour, a spirit of forgiveness, caring for the sick, concern for the poor, and the making of peace as did the earthly faith of Jesus.

Yet in spite of this heavy emphasis on the continuity between the Jesus of history and the Christ of faith it must be pointed out that there is also a definite dimension of discontinuity within this line of continuity. This important element of discontinuity can only properly be understood within the context of our above description of underlying personal continuity. As such this element of discontinuity does not in any way infringe upon the personal continuity which we have been describing. It does, however, concern our understanding of the mode of that personal continuity which exists between the Jesus of history and the Christ of faith. Obviously the mode of existence belonging to the risen Christ of faith is radically different and therefore discontinuous with the mode of historical existence which attached to the earthly life of Jesus. It is in this sense that there is a distinct dimension of discontinuity, a discontinuity which is specifically historical. The reality of the risen Christ of faith is unhistorical or better, trans-historical, and is therefore to that extent discontinuous with the Jesus of history.

This dimension of discontinuity can be seen in our discussion of the resurrection experiences. It will be remembered that alongside our emphasis on continuity there was also an equally strong emphasis on discontinuity. This was based on the evidence of Paul and those accounts by the Evangelists which tell us that the apostles initially failed to recognise the risen Jesus, that some even doubted that it was the risen Jesus, and that the risen Jesus "comes" and "goes" in a way no earthly body does. These reports bring out the change, the newness, and the transformation which took place in the resurrection of Jesus from the dead. Such qualities of discontinuity are derived from the theological fact that in and through the resurrection the Jesus of history is transformed into a new mode of existence, an eschatological mode of existence which lies outside time and space. It is this new mode of eschatological existence belonging to the risen Christ which gives rise to the historical discontinuity between the Jesus of history and the Christ of faith.

As in the case of personal continuity one can also detect different levels of discontinuity between the Jesus of history and the Christ of faith. On the eschatological level there is discontinuity in that the end of time has already occurred in the resurrection of Jesus and the new era has begun in Jesus as the risen Christ. The old which has passed away and the new which is yet to come universally is here in principle in the reigning Lordship of Jesus. The new future as promised is now grounded in the living reality of the risen Jesus who is "the first fruits" of God's universal eschatological harvest. The "new creation" in Jesus as the risen Christ is a blueprint or a preview event around which the future is presently being shaped. As a result of this initiation through Jesus as the risen Christ into these horizons of a new heaven and a new earth one can discover an eschatological discontinuity between the Jesus of history and the Christ of faith.

On the level of christology there is also a discontinuity between the Jesus of history and the Christ of faith in that the risen Christ reigns as universal Lord in a way that was impossible to the particularity of the Jesus of history. Through this Lordship Jesus not only assumes the functions of Yahweh but actually embodies these functions in his person as the one who sits at the right hand of the Father. In this way the universal reign of God diffuses itself in the world through the Lordship of Christ. It is in the light of this universal Lordship of Jesus that one must recognise the existence of a christological discontinuity between the Jesus of history and the Christ of faith.

Thirdly on the level of faith, there is a discontinuity between the Jesus of history and the Christ of faith insofar as the risen Christ has become the new object of faith which is now specifically called Christian Faith. As the object of faith Jesus Christ defines, personalises and concretises the content of basic faith in a new way. Christian faith provides basic faith with a new stance towards God, a stance which sees Jesus Christ as *the* mediator of the inexhaustible mystery we call God. We now know the *way* to God; it is the way through Jesus Christ our Lord who is the new object of our religious faith. It is as new object of faith that one discovers the discontinuity on the level of faith itself between the Jesus of history and the risen Christ.

In the light of this analysis of continuity and discontinuity we can say that the relationship between the Jesus of history and the Christ of faith is one of personal sameness within historical differentiation. The person referred to is one and the same reality whereas the mode of being belonging to this person has been changed historically. The historical pastness of Jesus has been transformed into the present living reality of Christ. The relation therefore between the Jesus of history and the Christ of faith is one of personal identity-within-radical-transformation. In a word there is a dynamic relationship of personal continuity within historical discontinuity between the Jesus of history and the Christ of faith.

Closely bound up with this issue of the relationship between the Jesus of history and the Christ of faith is the wider question of the relationship between history and faith. We can only refer briefly at the risk of over-simplification to this question, in so far as christology would seem to have something to say to it. In the light of our analysis of the historical foundations of the Christ-Event and our above discussion of the interplay between these historical foundations and the Christ of faith it would appear that one is justified in making the more general observation that faith is based on history and that history gives rise to faith. This should surely be clear by now in the case of Christian faith. Can the same be said about basic faith which is the preface to Christian faith? We would suggest that in fact it can in the sense that the personal history of man and his particular experiences within this history are the raw material out of which basic faith is born. Man exists within the world and it is through his experiences within that graced history that basic faith comes to be. As such these observations are primarily concerned with the genesis of faith. They are directed therefore towards the initial point of departure within basic faith. Once basic faith comes to be through historical experience then there will of course be a trans-historical dimension to it just as there is an element of discontinuity within Christian faith as founded upon the Jesus of history.

There can be no doubt that past approaches to the question of the Jesus of history and the Christ of faith which took place predominantly in Protestant circles were conditioned by a doctrinaire adherence to the Lutheran principle of justification by faith alone (*sola fide*).[17] Such adherence demanded that faith be in no way dependent on external reality be it human or historical. Faith was understood literally as an interior gift to man from God. Consequently it was required that faith be freed from all human endeavour.

It was out of this background that the dichotomy between the Jesus of history and the Christ of faith grew up and the resulting divorce between history and faith. This doctrinaire dichotomy is best exemplified in the once influential position of Bultmann. For Bultmann Christian faith exists independently of anything we can know about the life of the historical Jesus.[18] In fact the historical Jesus is irrelevant to the Christ of faith. To make faith in any way dependent on what we know about the historical Jesus, which for Bultmann in practice is not insignificant despite theoretical protestations to the contrary, would be to construct faith exclusively on scholarship. What matters for Bultmann in the realm of faith is "the Christ of the kerygma and not the person of Jesus".[19] Thus the Jesus of history becomes divorced from the Christ of faith with the implication that faith is unrelated to history.

Further approaches to this question of the Jesus of history and the Christ of faith will have to incorporate alongside the Protestant emphasis on the primacy of God's initiative in the process of faith, the equally important emphasis of the Catholic tradition which acknowledges the necessary role that man must play in the coming to be of faith. This Catholic tradition is summarised in its doctrine of "justification by faith and good works". This doctrine implies without prejudice to the priority of God's invitation that man must cooperate actively in the reception of the divine gift of faith. Part of this cooperation is to search out the approaches that God makes to man in history, especially the supreme approach which he has made to us in Jesus of Nazareth. It is not our intention here to resurrect old polemics. To the contrary we believe that the Protestant and the Catholic tradition when properly understood can complement each other in this respect. In particular they can together enrich and advance our understanding of God's invitation to man in history especially the historical manifestation of this invitation in Jesus Christ who is our Lord.

It is on this note concerning the importance of the historical dimension for faith that we wish to end this chapter and to bring to a close our reflections on the mystery of Jesus Christ. Our essay in christology began with a critical examination of the life, death, and resurrection of Jesus. It is appropriate that it should end by being drawn back to that historical life of Jesus as guide and norm. The search for God, when all is said and done, is a search within history both past and present. This search cannot afford to ignore "the reality of Jesus".

Notes

1 Introduction

1. HAHN, F., *The Titles of Jesus in Christology* (London: Lutter-worth Press, 1969), p. 192.
2. Quotations from Scripture are taken from *The Revised Standard Version, Common Bible* (London: Collins, 1973)
3. VAWTER B., *This Man Jesus* (New York: Doubleday & Company, Inc., 1973) p. 97.
4. *Ibid.*
5. CULLMANN, O., *The Christology of the New Testament* (London: S.C.M. Press, 1959), p. 111.
6. See also *1 Cor 12:3; Phil 2:9-11; 2 Cor 4:5; Acts 2:36-38.*
7. Docetism comes from the Greek verb *dokein* "to seem". It suggests that Jesus only "appeared" to have a real human body. Gnosticism comes from the Greek word *gnosis* meaning "knowledge". In the context of christology, it implies that Jesus was some kind of mystical figure who saved people by communicating to them a special knowledge.
8. Moralism is the view which reduces Jesus to just another moral figure in history. Adoptionism sees Jesus as one who, because he lives a good life, is adopted by God as his Son.
9. PANNENBERG, W., "Redemptive Event and History", *Basic Questions in Theology* (London: S.C.M. Press, 1970), Vol. 1, pp. 17-19.
10. GREEHY, J. J., "The People of God", *The Meaning of the Church* Flanagan (ed.), (Dublin: Gill & Son, 1965), pp. 1-17.
11. MOLTMANN, J., *Theology of Hope* (London: S.C.M. Press, 1967), pp. 99-100.
12. PANNENBERG, W., *Jesus—God and Man* (London: S.C.M. Press, 1968), p. 33.
13. BRAATEN, C., *Christ and Counter Christ* (Philadelphia: Fortress Press, 1972), p. 43.
14. ROBINSON, J. A. T., *The Human Face of God* (London: S.C.M. Press, 1973), p. 102.
15. Cf. the useful summary given by R. Brown in *The Virginal Conception and Bodily Resurrection of Jesus* (New York: Paulist Press, 1973), pp. 1-20.
16. Cf. PANNENBERG, W., "Introduction" *Revelation as History* W. Pannenberg (ed.) (London: Sheed and Ward, 1969), pp. 1-22.

17. Cf. RAHNER, K., "What is a Dogmatic Statement?" *Theological Investigations* 5 (London: D.L.T., 1962), pp. 42-66. Hereafter this series, volume one to twelve (1961-1974) will be abbreviated as *T.I.*
18. Cf. HODGSON, P. C., *Jesus—Lord and Presence* (Philadelphia: Fortress Press, 1971), pp. 60-70.
19. PANNENBERG, W., *Jesus—God and Man* pp. 34-35.
20. RAHNER, K., "Current Problems in Christology" *T.I. 1* p. 188.
21. PANNENBERG, W., *op. cit.*, p. 35.
22. BRAATEN, C., *op. cit.*, p. 43.
23. BONHOEFFER, D., *Letters and Papers from Prison* (The Enlarged Edition), E. Bethge (ed.). (London: S.C.M. Press, 1971), p. 381.
24. BRANDON, S. G. F., *Jesus and the Zealots* (Manchester: Manchester University Press, 1967).
25. HOLL, A., *Jesus in Bad Company* (London: Collins, 1972).
26. KEY, A., *The Way of Transcendence* (London: Penguin Books, 1971).
27. SÖLLE, D., *Christ the Representative* (London: S.C.M. Press, 1967).
28. COX, H., *Feast of Fools* (Cambridge: C.U.P., 1969).
29. Cf. MORAN, G., *The Present Revelation* (New York: Herder & Herder, 1973), ch. 2.
30. KNOX, J., *The Humanity and Divinity of Jesus* (Cambridge: C.U.P. 1967), pp. 1-18.

2 The historical Jesus and biblical research

1. BRAATEN, C., *History and Hermeneutics* (Philadelphia: The Westminster Press, 1966), p. 55.
2. TILLICH, P., *The New Being* (London: S.C.M. Press, 1956), p. 99.
3. TILLICH, P., *Systematic Theology 2* (Chicago: The University Press of Chicago, 1957), p. 105.
4. BULTMANN, R., *Jesus and the Word* (New York: Scribner, 1958), p. 8ff.
5. Cf. BROWN, R., "After Bultmann, What?—An Introduction to the Post-Bultmannians". *Catholic Biblical Quarterly* Vol. 26, 1964, pp. 1-30.
6. ROBINSON, J. M., "The Recent Debate on the 'New Quest'." *Journal of Bible and Religion 30* 1962, pp. 198-208.
7. ROBINSON, J. M., "Basic Shifts in German Theology." *Interpretation 16* 1962, pp. 76-97.
8. EBELING, G., *Theology and Proclamation* (Philadelphia: Fortress Press, 1966), p. 91.
9. PANNENBERG, W., *Jesus—God and Man* pp. 50, 58.
10. BRAATEN, C., *History and Hermeneutics* p. 11ff.
11. *Dogmatic Constitution on Divine Revelation* Ch 5. Quotations

from the Second Vatican Council will be taken from *The Documents of Vatican II* Abbott (ed.). (London: Chapman, 1966.)

12. *The Historical Truths of the Gospels* Sec. 2. Available in *The Irish Ecclesiastical Record* July 1964, pp. 44-51.
13. *Ibid.*
14. *Ibid.*
15. *Ibid.*
16. *Ibid.*
17. *Ibid.*
18. FITZMYER, J. A., "The Biblical Commission's Instruction on the Historical Truth of the Gospels," *Theological Studies* 2 1964, p. 401.
19. COLLINGWOOD, R. G., *The Idea of History* (Oxford: Clarendon Press, 1946), p. 10ff, p. 182ff.
20. ROBINSON, C. K., "Historical Methodology and Biblical Hermeneutic" *The Duke Divinity School Review* Spring 1969, p. 81ff.
21. PANNENBERG, W., "Dogmatic Theses on the Concept of Revelation." *Revelation as History* W. Pannenberg (ed.), p. 152.
22. a.2., brackets added.
23. A helpful discussion of these criteria may be found in: R. Bultmann *History of the Synoptic Tradition* (New York: Harper & Row., 1963), p. 265; R. H. Fuller *The New Testament in Current Study* (London: S.C.M. Press), p. 40ff; R. S. Barbour, *Traditio-Historical Criticism of the Gospels* (London: S.P.C.K. 1972), p. 3ff.
24. CALVERT, D. H., "An Examination of the Criteria for Distinguishing the Authentic Teaching of Jesus." *New Testament Studies 19* 1973, pp. 271-283.
25. These three strands have been exposed particularly by HAHN, F., *op. cit.* and FULLER, R. H., *The Foundations of New Testament Christology* (London: Lutterworth Press, 1965).

3 Rediscovering the historical Jesus

1. We do not intend to be drawn here or elsewhere into the largely unprofitable debate about the knowledge and consciousness of Jesus. We take it as axiomatic that Jesus as a man grew in knowledge and self-understanding in the same way as any other man grows in knowledge and self-understanding. Over and above this basic point no one can afford to be too dogmatic. Cf. RAHNER, K., "Dogmatic Reflections on the Knowledge and Self-consciousness of Christ." *T.I. 5*, pp. 193-218.
2. DODD, C. H., *The Founder of Christianity* (London: Collins, 1971), pp. 53-80.
3. On this category see WANSBROUGH, H., "The Mission of Jesus. II: The Prophet." *The Clergy Review* July 1972, pp 513-522.

G

4. SCHELKLE, K. H., *Discipleship and Priesthood* (London: Sheed & Ward, 1964), pp. 9-32.
5. Cf. the helpful exposition on miracles by MAHER, M., "Miracles and Miracle Stories." *Scripture in Church* Nos. 9, 12, 15.
6. SCHLIER, H., *Theological Dictionary of the New Testament* Vol. 1. KITTEL G. and BROMILEY, G. W. (tr. and ed.) (Michigan: Wm. B. Berdmans Publishing Company, 1964), p. 338.
7. PERRIN, N., *Rediscovering the Teaching of Jesus* (London: S.C.M. Press, 1967), pp. 102-108.
8. JEREMIAS, J., *New Testament Theology* Part One (London: S.C.M. Press, 1971), pp. 250-255.
9. JEREMIAS, J., *The Prayers of Jesus* S.B.T. (London: S.C.M. Press, 1967), pp. 11-65.
10. The situating of the historical Jesus within an apocalyptic framework is one of the basic characteristics of the "Pannenberg Circle". Cf. WILCKENS, U., "The Understanding of Revelation Within the History of Primitive Christianity." *Revelation as History* pp. 57-121.
11. BRAATEN, C., *Christ and Counter Christ* p. 7.
12. PANNENBERG, W., *Jesus—God and Man* pp. 58-66.
13. BULTMANN, R., *Jesus and the Word* p. 124.
14. On this category of "eschatological prophet" see: CULLMANN, O., *The Christology of the New Testament* pp. 13-38. FULLER, R. H., *The Foundations of the New Testament Christology* pp. 46-49. LONGENECKER, R. N., *The Christology of Early Jewish Christianity* S.B.T. (London: S.C.M. Press, 1970), pp. 32-38.
15. PANNENBERG, W., *op. cit.* pp. 64-66.
16. JEREMIAS, J., *op. cit.* p. 278.
17. BORNKAMM, G., *Jesus of Nazareth* (London: Hodder and Stoughton, 1960), pp. 154-158.
18. For a discussion of some of the problems involved in this question see VAWTER, B., *This Man Jesus* pp. 64-68.
19. Cf. *Is 42:1-4; 49:1-7; 50:4-11; 52:13; 53:12.*

4 The resurrection: a survey of the evidence

1. A helpful discussion of these verses may be found in: SMITH, J. J., "Resurrection Faith Today." *Theological Studies* Sept. 1969, pp. 403-410; RIGAUX, B., *Dieu l'a ressucité* (Belgium: Duculot, 1973), pp. 119-146.
2. Favoured by JEREMIAS, J., *The Eucharist Words of Jesus* (Oxford: Blackwell, 1955), pp. 30-130.
3. Implied by CONZELMANN, H., "An Analysis of the Confessional Formula of *1 Cor 15:3-5.*" *Interpretation* 20 1966, pp. 15-25.
4. PANNENBERG, W., "Did Jesus Really Rise from the Dead?" *New Testament Issues* Batey (ed.). (London: S.C.M. Press, 1970), p. 104.

5. *1 Cor 15:16.*
6. DAVIES, W. D., *Paul and Rabbinic Judaism* 1955), pp. 299-303.
7. To appreciate this contrast, it is imper damaging dualism which sees man simpl which separate at death. For the Hebrew made up of different dimensions such a flesh.
8. On this difficult question see: CARREZ, M., "With What Do the Dead Rise?" *Concilium* Dec. 1970, pp. 92-102; AUDET, L., "Avec Quel Corps Les Justes Ressuciteront-ils?" *Résurrection* (Audet et alia). (Montréal: Bellarmin, 1971), pp. 27-47.
9. FULLER, R. H., *The Formation of the Resurrection Narratives* (New York: The Macmillan Co., 1971), pp. 16-18.
10. HAIIN, F., *The Titles of Jesus in Christology* p. 181.
11. LEON-DUFOUR, X., "Appearances and Hermeneutics." *The Resurrection and Modern Biblical Thought* DE SURGY, P. (ed.). (New York: Corpus Books, 1970), p. 121.
12. MOULE, C. F. D., "Introduction." *The significance of the Message of the Resurrection for Faith in Jesus Christ* S.B.T., MOULE (ed.). (London: S.C.M. Press, 1968), p. 28.
13. BROWN, R., "The Resurrection and Biblical Criticism." *Commonweal* 24 Nov. 1967, p. 233.
14. BROWN, R., *art. cit.*, pp. 233-234; O'COLLINS, G., *The Easter Jesus* (London: D.L.T., 1973), pp. 22-23.
15. PANNENBERG, W., *art. cit.*, p. 109; BROWN, R., *The Virginal Conception and Bodily Resurrection* pp. 102-106.
16. This pattern has been detected independently by the following two authors: LEON-DUFOUR, X., *Résurrection de Jésus et message pascal* (Paris: Édition du Seuil, 1971), pp. 126-130; DODD, C. H., "The Appearances of the Risen Christ: A study in Form-Criticism of the Gospels." *More New Testament Studies* (Manchester: M.U.P., 1968), pp. 104-107.
17. BROWN, R., *op. cit.*, p. 89.
18. It is instructive to note here that this "physicalising" tendency is more prominent in Luke and John, who were in fact writing to Greek communities.
19. BROWN, R., *op. cit.*, p. 111.
20. BROWN, R., "The Resurrection and Biblical Criticism." *Commonweal* 24 Nov. 1967, p. 234.
21. WILCKENS, U., "Tradition-history of the Resurrection of Jesus." *The Significance of the Message of the Resurrection for Faith in Jesus Christ* Moule (ed.), p. 73.
22. BROWN, R., *art. cit.*, p. 234.
23. MARXSEN, W., *The Resurrection of Jesus of Nazareth* (London: S.C.M. Press, 1970), p. 161; EVELY, L., *The Gospels Without Myth* (New York: Doubleday), pp. 84, 97-99.
24. PANNENBERG, W., *art. cit.*, p. 113.

DELORME, J., "The Resurrection and Jesus' Tomb." *The Resurrection and Modern Biblical Thought* de Surgy (ed.), p. 103.

26. O'COLLINS, G., *Foundations of Theology* (Chicago: Loyola University Press, 1966), p. 167.

27. MARXSEN, W., *The Resurrection of Jesus of Nazareth* (London: S.C.M. Press, 1970), p. 77.

28. VAN BUREN, P., *The Secular Meaning of the Gospel* (London: S.C.M. Press, 1963), pp. 133, 169.

29. WALKER, WM. O. JR., "Christian Origins and Resurrection Faith." *Journal of Religion* Jan. 1972, pp. 41-55.

30. MOULE, C. F. D., "Introduction." *The Significance of the Message of the Resurrection for Faith in Jesus Christ* Moule (ed.), p. 9.

31. See our treatment in Chapter II, section (b).

32. O'COLLINS, G., *The Easter Jesus* pp. 64, 69, 133.

33. BROWN, R., *op. cit.*, pp. 89-92, 100; RAHNER, K., "The Position of Christology in the Church between Exegesis and Dogmatics." *T.I. 11*, p. 208.

34. LEON-DUFOUR, X., *op. cit.*, pp. xiii-xxii.

5 The mystery of the resurrection: a theological response

1. GRELOT, P., "The Resurrection of Jesus: Its Biblical and Jewish Background." *The Resurrection and Modern Biblical Thought* Surgy (ed.), pp. 8-10.

2. DAVIES, W. D., *Paul and Rabbinic Judaism* p. 300ff.

3. MOLTMANN, J., *Theology of Hope* pp. 99-120.

4. His reply reflects the influence of Jewish apocalyptic thought upon his own understanding of Resurrection. *See 1 Enoch 51:4* "In those days mountains will leap like rams and the hills will abound like milk-fed lambs; and all the righteous will be *like angels in heaven*." (Emphasis added.)

5. GRELOT, P., *art. cit.*, pp. 20-23.

6. FULLER, R. H., *The Formation of the Resurrection Narratives* p. 60. It is now generally agreed that the Passion Prophecies, *Mk 8:31; 9:31; 10:32-34*) which predict the individual resurrection of Jesus, have been written up in the light of the Easter Event. Cf. HAHN F., *op. cit.*, p. 37ff; BORNKAMM *op. cit.*, p. 229ff; PANNENBERG, W., *op. cit.*, p. 65; BROWN, R., *Jesus God and Man* (London: Chapman, 1968), p. 61ff; RIGAUX, B., *Dieu l'a ressucité* pp. 194-195.

7. FREYNE, S., "The Meaning of the Resurrection of Jesus." *Scripture in Church No. 6* pp. 420-428.

8. PANNENBERG, W., *op. cit.*, p. 17.

9. MOULE, C. F. D., *art. cit.*, p. 9.

10. PANNENBERG, W., *op. cit.*, p. 69.

11. VON RAD, G., *Old Testament Theology* Vol. II (London: Oliver & Boyd, 1965), p. 100ff.
12. The Resurrection plays a key role in the current theologies of liberation. Cf. BOFF, L., *Jesus Christ Libérateur* (Paris: Les éditions du Cerf, 1974), Ch. 7.
13. FULLER, R. H., *The Foundations of New Testament Christology* p. 143ff.
14. *Ibid.*, pp. 156-157.
15. *Ibid.*, p. 159.
16. *Ibid.*, pp. 162-165.
17. LONGENECKER, R. N., *The Christology of Early Jewish Christianity* p. 94.
18. LONGENECKER, R. N., *op. cit.*, pp. 32-38; FULLER, R. H., *op. cit.*, pp. 167-173.
19. FULLER, R. H., *op. cit.*, pp. 184-186.
20. FULLER, R. H., *op. cit.*, p. 201ff: KNOX, J., *The Humanity and Divinity of Jesus*, pp. 1-18.

6 Discovering the implications of the Christ-Event

1. See Chapter 3 for a more detailed account of these different points.
2. The 1964 Instruction on *The Historical Truth of the Gospels*, sec. 2; *The Dogmatic Constitution on Divine Revelation—The Documents of Vatican II* Abbott (ed.), a. 19.
3. HAHN, F., *op. cit.*, p. 79.
4. VAWTER, B., *This Man Jesus*, p. 101.
5. *Ibid.*, p. 100.
6. CULLMANN, O., *The Christology of the New Testament* p. 202.
7. FULLER, R. H., *The Foundations of New Testament Christology* p. 50; CULLMANN, O., *op. cit.*, p. 201ff.
8. HAHN, F., *op. cit.*, p. 97.
9. FULLER, R. H., *op. cit.*, p. 68.
10. VAWTER, B., *op. cit.*, pp. 101-102.
11. HAHN, F., *op. cit.*, p. 105.
12. FULLER, R. H., *op. cit.*, p. 68.
13. *Ibid.*, p. 186; HAHN, F., *op. cit.*, p. 109.
14. It is important to remember here that a name is more than a label; it is the expression of a person's nature and being.
15. BROWN, R., *Jesus God and Man*, p. 33.
16. RAHNER, K., "Theos in the New Testament." *T.I. 1*, pp. 125-130.
17. LONGENECKER, R. N., *op. cit.*, p. 137.
18. BARRETT, C. K., *The Gospel According to St John* (London: S.P.C.K., 1956), p. 476.
19. CULLMANN, O., *op. cit.*, p. 308. BROWN, R., *op. cit.*, p. 23ff.
20. BROWN, R., *op cit.*, pp. 13-23, provides a careful examination of these probable instances.

21. BROWN, R., *op. cit.*, pp. 35-36.
22. OWEN, H. P., "The New Testament and the Incarnation: A Study in Doctrinal Development." *Religious Studies 8* 1972, pp. 229-230.
23. ROBINSON, J. A. T., *The Human Face of God*, p. 180. ROBINSON, J. A. T., "The Use of the Fourth Gospel for Christology Today." *Christ and Spirit in the New Testament* Linders and Smalley (eds.). (Cambridge: C.U.P. 1973), pp. 68-75.
24. E.g.: "What father among you, if his son asks for a fish, will instead of a fish give him a serpent. . . . How much more will the Heavenly Father give . . ." *Lk 11:11-13*.
25. BARRETT, C. K., *op. cit.*, p. 60.
26. FULLER, R. H., *op. cit.*, p. 231. LONGENECKER, R. N., *op. cit.*, p. 140.
27 It was this christological breakthrough that gave rise to the Christian doctrine of the Tri-Unity of God

7 Defining the universal significance of the Christ-Event

1. HANSON, R. P. C., *The Attractiveness of God* (London S.P.C.K., 1973), p. 76.
2. Transformation, as distinct from destruction, always implies a line of continuity between the *terminus a quo* and the *terminus ad quem*.
3. WILES, M., *The Christian Fathers* (London: Hodder and Stoughton, 1966), p. 25.
4. JENKINS, D. E., *The Glory of Man* (London S.C.M. Press, 1967), p. 38ff.
5. CULLMANN, O., *op. cit.*, p. 251; DODD, C. H., *The Interpretation of the Fourth Gospel* (Cambridge: C.U.P., 1953), pp. 133, 263, 277-280; FULLER, R. H., *op. cit.*, p. 76.
6. SMULDERS, P., *The Fathers on Christology* (Wisconsin: St Norbert Abbey Press, 1968), pp. 58-60.
7. Taken from SMULDERS, *op. cit.*, p. 72.
8. TILLICH, P., *A History of Christian Thought* C. Braaten (ed.). (London: S.C.M. Press, 1968), p. 72.
9. WILES, M., "The Doctrine of Christ in the Patristic Age." *Christ for Us Today* (London: S.C.M. Press, 1968), p. 85.
10. Taken from SMULDERS, *op. cit.*, p. 87.
11. WILES, M., *The Making of Christian Doctrine* (Cambridge: C.U.P. 1967), Ch. 3.
12. Taken from SMULDERS, *op. cit.*, p. 96.
13. SMULDERS, P., *op. cit.*, pp. 99-100.
14. SMULDERS, P., *op. cit.*, p. 112-119.
15. *The Teaching of the Catholic Church* K. Rahner (ed.). Co piled by Roos and Neuner (Cork: Mercier Press, 1967), p. 1

16. Taken from SMULDERS, *op. cit.*, p. 134.
17. RAHNER, K., "Current Problems in Christology." *T.I. 1*, pp. 149-200 (Original German title of this article was "Chalcedon—Ende oder Anfang?"); GRILLMIER, A., *Christ in Christian Tradition* (London: A. R. Mowbray & Co. Ltd., 1965), pp. 492-495.

8 Reshaping the christological dogma

1. SCHLEIERMACHER, F., *The Christian Faith 2* (New York: Harper & Row, 1963), p. 392ff.
2. RAHNER, K., "Current Problems in Christology." *T.I. 1*, pp. 149-200; NORTH, R., *In Search of the Human Jesus* (New York: Corpus Papers, 1970), pp. 1-63. (This little book summarises the views of A. Hulsbosch, P. Schoonenberg and E. Schillebeeckx on Christology with particular reference to the traditional language of Chalcedon); SCHOONENBERG, P., *The Christ* (New York: Herder & Herder, 1971), pp. 51-104; MOONEY, C., "Christology and the American Experience." *Proceedings of the Catholic Theological Society of America*, 1972, pp. 48-53. SLOYAN, G., "Some Problems in Modern Christology." *A World More Human—A Church More Christian* (New York: Alba House, 1973), pp. 27-51.
3. PRESTIGE, G. L., *God in Patristic Thought* (London: S.P.C.K., 1952), p. 197ff.
4. HICK, J., "Christology at the Cross Roads." *Prospect for Theology* Healey (ed.). (London: J. Nisbet & Co. Ltd., 1966), p. 151.
5. Cf. the I.C.E.L. new English translation of the Creed and commentary by PETER, C. J., "A New Challenge From an Old Creed." *Worship* March 1973, pp. 150-154.
6. See SCHILLEBEECKX E., *The Eucharist* (London: Sheed & Ward, 1968), pp. 53-76.
7. This classical definition goes back to Boethius of the seventh century.
8. RAHNER, K., "Jesus Christ." *Sacramentum Mundi 3*, p. 196.
9. WALKER, J. B., *New Theology for Plain Christians* (New Jersey: Dimension Books, 1971), p. 30; GROOF, W. F., *Christ, the Hope of the Future* (Michigan: W. B. Eerdmans Publishing Co., 1971), p. 93; VAWTER, B., *This Man Jesus* (New York: Doubleday and Company Inc., 1973), p. 146.
10. RAHNER, K., "Current Problems in Christology." *T.I. 1*, pp. 160-161; "Jesus Christ." *Sacramentum Mundi 3*, p. 206; BEGGIANI, S., "A Case for Logocentric Christology." *Theological Studies*, Sept. 1971, p. 401; BUTLER, C., "Bishop Robinson's Christ." *Heythrop Journal* Oct. 1973, p. 429.
11. TILLICH, P., *Systematic Theology* Vol. 1, p. 142; MACQUARRIE, J., *Principles of Christian Theology*, p. 273; VAWTER, B., *op. cit.*, p. 148.

12. The Theology Commission of the Hierarchy of England and Wales, *Who is Jesus Christ?* (London: C.T.S., 1973), p. 7; JENKINS, D., *The Glory of Man*, p. 67.

13. Cf. footnote 10 above.

14. RAHNER, K., "Current Problems in Christology", *T.I. 1*, p. 159; BEGGIANI, S., *art. cit.*, pp. 399, 401.

15. A discussion of this point may be found in RAHNER, K., *art. cit.*, p. 159.

16. GLASSER, J. W., "Man's Existence: Supernatural Relation." *Theological Studies* Sept. 1969, p. 478; RAHNER, K., "Reflections on the Unity of the Love of Neighbour and the Love of God." *T.I. 6*, p. 244.

17. A possible exception to this would be the phenomenon of "mystical experience". Even here, however, it is instructive to note that most mystics appear to be very involved with the world around them within their "mystical experience". This can be seen from the imagery which they use to describe their experience.

18. RAHNER, K., "The Experience of God Today." *T.I. 11*, pp. 149-165.

19. *Summa Theologica* 1, q. 12, a. 11.

20. SCHOONENBERG, P., "God's Presence in Jesus: an exchange of viewpoints." *Theology Digest* Spring 1971, p. 30; NORTH, R., *In Search of the Humc Jesus* pp. 13, 33, 36, 41.

21. NORTH, R., *op. cit.*, pp. 32-33.

22. JENKINS, D., *op. cit.*, pp. 67-68.

23. PANNENBERG, W., *Jesus—God and Man*, p. 342.

24. Australian Episcopal Conference *The Renewal of the Education of Faith* (Sydney: E. J. Dwyer, 1970), p. 98. This document is a translation of *Il Rinnovamento della Catechesi* published by the Italian Episcopal Conference. It has recently (1974) been adopted also by the English Episcopal Conference.

25. The Theology Commission of the Hierarchy of England and Wales *Who is Jesus Christ?* p. 8.

26. HULSBOSCH, A. in NORTH, R., *In Search of the Human Jesus* p.15.

27. RAHNER, K., "Current Problems in Christology." *T.I. 1*, p. 184.

28. Congregation for the Clergy, Rome *General Catechetical Directory* (London C.T.S., 1971), sec. 53.

29. RAHNER, K., *Ibid.* "Theology and Anthropology." *T.I. 9*, p. 28ff.

30. RAHNER, K., in *Encyclopedia of Theology* Rahner (ed.). (London: Burns and Oates, 1975), p. 1589.

31. LAMPE, G. W. H., "The Saving Work of Christ." *Christ for Us Today* p. 143.

32. FANNON, P., "The Apostles Creed Revisited: II." *The Clergy Review* March 1974, p. 177.

33. SCHOONENBERG, P., *op. cit.*, p. 142.

34. MACQUARRIE, J., *Principles of Christian Theology* p. 277.

35. ROBINSON, J. A. T., *The Human Face of God* pp. 155-156.

36. CULLMANN, O., *op. cit.*, p. 176; ROBINSON, J. A. T., *op. cit.*, pp. 163-164.
37. *Pastoral Constitution on the Church in the Modern World* a. 22.
38. RAHNER, K., "Jesus Christ." *Sacramentum Mundi,* p. 196; "Cardinal vs Theologian" (Correspondence between J. Hoffner and K. Rahner) *The Month* April 1971, pp. 104-107.
39. This is what the complicated, though important, doctrine about the *communicatio idiomatum* was trying to say. See *Concise Theological Dictionary* Rahner and Vorgrimler (eds.). (London : Burns & Oates, 1965), p. 90.
40. PANNENBERG, W., *What is Man?* (Philadelphia : Fortress Press, 1970), pp. 1-13.
41. RAHNER, K., *Hearers of the Word* (New York : Herder & Herder, 1969), pp. 31-68.
42. LONGERGAN, P., *Insight: A Study of Human Understanding* (New York : Longmans, 1958, Students' Edition), Ch. XIX.
43. TILLICH, P., *Systematic Theology 1* pp. 163-210.
44. SCHILLEBEECKX, E., *God and Man* (London : Sheed and Ward, 1969), p. 216.
45. RAHNER, K., "On the Theology of Incarnation." *T.I. 4,* pp. 105-120; "Incarnation." *Sacramentum Mundi 3,* pp. 114-118.

9 Relocating the dogma of the Incarnation

1. RAHNER, K., "On the Theology of Incarnation." *T.I. 4,* pp. 119-120; "Christology within an Evolutionary View." *T.I. 5,* pp. 175-176; "Christology in the Setting of Modern Man's Understanding of Himself and of His World." *T.I. 11,* pp. 226-227.
2. PITTENGER, N., *The Word Incarnate* (London : Nisbet, 1959), p. 188.
3. GRAY, D. P., "The Incarnation : God's Giving and Man's Receiving." *New Horizons* Fall 1974, pp. 1-13.
4. BAILLIE, D. M., *God Was in Christ* (London : Faber and Faber Ltd., 1956), pp. 114-118.
5. RAHNER, K., "Current Problems in Christology." *T.I. 1,* p. 162; RAHNER, K. and VORGRIMLER, H., *Concise Theological Dictionary* p. 219.
6. HAMILTON, P., in *The Living God and the Modern World* (Philadelphia : United Church Press 1967) points out that "enormous differences of degree . . . can amount to a difference of kind : this is highly relevant to our question about Christ." p. 208. Cf. also GRAY, D. P., *art. cit.*, pp. 11-12.
7. ROBINSON, J. A. T., "Need Jesus Have Been Perfect?" *Christ, Faith, and History* Sykes and Clayton (eds.). (Cambridge : C.U.P., 1972), p. 39.

174 THE REALITY OF JESUS

8. *General Catechetical Directory*, sec. 51 and the helpful commentary by MARTHALER, B. L., *Catechesis in Context* (Indiana: Our Sunday Visitor, Inc., 1973), pp. 99, 101.
9. RAHNER, K., "Christology Within an Evolutionary Outlook." *T.I. 5*, pp. 177-178.
10. RAHNER, K., "Current Problems in Christology." *T.I. 1*, pp. 164-165.
11. *"Against Heresies"* in *The Ante-Nicene Fathers*, Vol. 1, Roberts and Donaldson (eds.). (Michigan: Eerdmans, 1953), 4.38,1.
12. A key figure here is T. de Chardin. Cf. BRAVO, F., *Christ in the Thought of Teilhard de Chardin* (Notre Dame: University of Notre Dame Press, 1967).
13. T. de Chardin wrote in 1948: "There is no creation without incarnational immersion." Cf. BRAVO, F., *op. cit.*, p. 38.
14. GRAY, D. P., "The Place of Jesus in Man's Becoming." *The Ecumenist* March-April 1972, pp. 41-44.
15. RAHNER, K., "Current Problems in Christology." *T.I. 1* pp. 164-165.
16. RAHNER, K., "Christology in the Setting of Modern Man's Understanding of Himself and of his World" *T.I. 11*, p. 220.
17. RAHNER, K., "On the Theology of the Incarnation." *T.I. 4*, p. 117.
18. DE CHARDIN, T., *Le Milieu Divin* (London: Fontana Books, 1964), p. 66.
19. RAHNER, K., "The Theology of Symbol." *T.I. 4*, p. 239.
20. a. 22 (emphasis added); cf. also a. 32.
21. MACQUARRIE, J., *Principles of Christian Faith*, p. 276.
22. For a clear and comprehensive treatment of the moral implications of christology see MURRAY, D., *Jesus is Lord* (Dublin: Veritas Publications, 1973).
23. Cf. *Decree on the Church; Missionary Activity of the Church. The Documents of Vatican II* a. 6.
24. *Dogmatic Constitution of the Church. The Documents of Vatican II* a. 8.
25. *Ibid*, a. 48 *Decree on the Missionary Activity of the Church* a. 1, 5.
26. RAHNER, K., "Christology in the Setting of Modern Man's Understanding of Himself and of His World." *T.I. 11*, p. 228.
27. DE CHARDIN, T., *Christianity and Evolution* (New York: Harper and Row, 1971), p. 53.
28. *Pastoral Constitution on the Church in the Modern World, The Documents of Vatican II* a. 22.
29. DULLES, A., "Incarnation." *Commonweal* 28 Dec. 1973, p. 336.
30. Cf. HAMILTON, W., *The New Essence of Christianity* (New York: Association Press, 1961); ALTIZER, T., *The Gospel of Christian Atheism* (Philadelphia: The Westminster Press, 1966).
31. RAHNER, K., "The Concept of Mystery in Catholic Thought." *T.I. 4*, pp. 48-49.
32. ROBINSON, J. A. T., *The Human Face of God* pp. 6-7, 23.
33. MACQUARRIE, J., *Principles of Christian Theology* pp. 232, 249.

34. BROWN, R., *The Gospel According to John* XIII-XXI (London: Chapman, 1971), pp. 620-621.
35. BAKER, J. A., "Behaviour as a Criterion of Membership." *Church Membership and Intercommunion* Kent and Murray (eds.). (London: D.L.T., 1973), p. 134.

10 A return to the historical roots of christology in Jesus

1. NEWBIGIN, G., *The Finality of Christ* (London: S.C.M. Press, 1969), p. 50.
2. DUQUOC, CH., *Christologie, I* (Paris: Les Éditions du Cerf, 1968), p. 107.
3. VAWTER, B., *op. cit.*, p. 152.
4. KITTEL, G., "The Jesus of History." *Mysterium Christi* Bell and Deissmann (eds.). (London: Longmans, Green, 1930), p. 40.
5. RAHNER, K., "Current Problems in Christology." *T.I. 1*, p. 188.
6. KECH, L. E., *A Future for the Historical Jesus* (London: S.C.M. Press, 1972), pp. 36-37.
7. DULLES, A., "Jesus of History and Christ of Faith." *Commonweal* 24 Nov. 1967, p. 222.
8. *The Historical Truth of the Gospels* sec. 2.
9. *Dogmatic Constitution on Divine Revelation* a. 4 (emphasis added).
10. E.g., EBELING, G., *Theology and Proclamation* (Philadelphia: Fortress Press, 1966), p. 91.
11. EBELING, G., *op. cit.*, p. 64; KÄSEMANN, E., "The Problem of the Historical Jesus." *Essays on New Testament Themes* (London: S.C.M. Press, 1964), p. 33ff; ROBINSON, J. M., *A New Quest of the Historical Jesus* (S.T.B.). (London, S.C.M. Press, 1959), p. 88.
12. BRAATEN, C., *History and Hermeneutics* p. 62.
13. O'COLLINS, G., *The Easter Jesus* Ch. 8.
14. DUQUOC, CH., *Christologie, II*, (Paris: Les Éditions du Cerf, 1972), p. 16.
15. SCHLIER, H., *Theological Dictionary of the New Testament* Vol. 1., p. 338, writes that "the whole of Christology is contained *in nuce*" in Jesus' use of Amen.
16. This level of continuity has been opened up helpfully by MACKEY, J. P., "Jesus in the New Testament: A Bibliographical Survey." *New Horizons* Fall 1974, pp. 51-73.
17. JENSEN, R. W., "Once More: The Jesus of History and the Christ of Faith." *Dialog* Spring 1972, pp. 118-124.
18. BULTMANN, R., *Theology of the New Testament* Vol. 1 (London: S.C.M. Press, 1952), p. 26.
19. BULTMANN, R., "The Primitive Christian Kerygma and the Historical Jesus." *The Historical Jesus and the Kerygmatic Christ* Braaten and Harrisville (eds.). (New York: Abingdon, 1964), p. 30.

Index of subjects

176